Praise for

The Mountains Are Calling

"What an incredible book to walk us through the mountaintop experiences God gave to so many of his saints in Scripture. If you've longed for a new kind of intimacy with God, a fresh experience of who he is and what he wants for you, this book is for you. It will, as Jarrett Stephens promises, change your perspective, first on who God is and second on who you are. You'll love this book!"

—J. D. GREEAR, PhD, pastor of The Summit Church, Raleigh-Durham, NC

"Most of us have had a mountaintop experience that quickly loses its luster or exhausts its energy. In *The Mountains Are Calling*, Jarrett Stephens will equip and empower you to recognize God's hand in those spiritual moments that can be a catalyst for your growth. Whether you are literally going to the mountains or just putting aside time for God, Jarrett will show you how God can use it."

—KYLE IDLEMAN, pastor and author of *Not a Fan* and *Grace Is Greater*

"To read *The Mountains Are Calling* is one of the best investments you can make for your soul. Jarrett Stephens charges us not only to take advantage of our mountaintop times with God but also to allow those experiences to permeate our lives and the lives of those around us. If you have an insatiable desire to understand more about God and who you are in light of him, this book is for you!"

—LEVI LUSKO, pastor of Fresh Life Church and author of
Swipe Right and *Through the Eyes of a Lion*

"I have known and loved Jarrett Stephens for a decade and recommend without reservation his book, *The Mountains Are Calling.* Behind the pen of these printed pages is a life of unquestioned character and a spotless reputation. Read it and reap! It will take you to new heights in your own spiritual journey."

—O. S. HAWKINS, president and CEO of GuideStone
Financial Resources and author of *The Joshua Code* and
the Code series

"I highly recommend this book no matter where you are on your faith journey. Jarrett writes with clarity and transparency. It's an honor to call him my friend and pastor. My life has been made richer because of this godly man."

—SHEILA WALSH, author of *It's Okay Not to Be Okay*

"Reading *The Mountains Are Calling,* coupled with Jarrett's teachings, I've learned that the only way our family will get to the mountain God is calling us to is on our knees."

—KALEB CANALES, New York Knicks assistant coach

"There's something about exploration that's always fascinated me. The greatest explorers learn that when the climber achieves the mountain peak, it makes all the difficulty, challenge, and pain it took to get there worthwhile. In *The Mountains Are Calling*, Jarrett Stephens captures exactly what that means for a Christian today. How do we conquer the mountains we're faced with, and what can God reveal to us as we see the world from that vantage point? While we can't always live on the mountain, the moments we spend there make the journey worthwhile. Get this book. It will challenge your thinking about moving beyond your limits and give you a new vision for what God can accomplish with your life."

—PHIL COOKE, PHD, filmmaker, media consultant, and
author of *The Way Back: How Christians Blew Our
Credibility and How We Get It Back*

"Mountaintops are both rugged and inspirational. Jarrett Stephens has done an excellent job unveiling biblical summits in an applicable way to those of us who feel like we are trudging through the valley most days. Let Jarrett be your climbing guide as you hike upward to discover more about yourself and, more importantly, about the Maker of the mountains."

—GREGG MATTE, pastor of Houston's First Baptist
Church and author of *Unstoppable Gospel*

"Jarrett Stephens is one of my heroes! He not only loves God and people—he lives it out in the way he invests in others. In his book, *The Mountains Are Calling*, Jarrett guides us on a journey to meet God, increase our self-awareness, and discover how we can best serve others. This book is a game changer and leaves me eagerly anticipating his future books!"

—CALEB KALTENBACH, author of *Messy Grace* and *God of Tomorrow*

"If you are longing for a mountaintop experience with God, I urge you to choose Jarrett Stephens as your sherpa. In his book, *The Mountains Are Calling,* Jarrett takes you on a hike full of affection-stirring page turns. You will see, with great clarity, the life lessons that God teaches us from the high places in Scripture. This book is for anyone who seeks to know and love God more."

—JONATHAN POKLUDA, teaching pastor of Watermark Community Church and The Porch and author of *Welcome to Adulting*

"Transforming moments occur on mountains. In this motivating book by my friend Jarrett Stephens, you will discover that when God *brings* you to a mountain in your life, he *will* see you through. Battles, decision-making, and greater faith always await you on the mountain. When you read this book, you will be ready to ascend the mountain, experience God, and then descend the mountain with a vision to change the world."

—DR. RONNIE FLOYD, senior pastor of Cross Church, president of the National Day of Prayer, and past president of the Southern Baptist Convention

"The message of this book is paramount for our souls. In *The Mountains Are Calling*, Jarrett Stephens has successfully parlayed his gift for teaching the Scriptures from the pulpit to the printed page. I highly recommend you make the *climb* with him through this incisive and powerful invitation to intimacy with God. You'll be glad you did."

—MICHAEL NEALE, national best-selling author and Dove Award–winning songwriter

"Jarrett is a great friend and a wonderful pastor. I love the heart of *The Mountains Are Calling*, urging us to break away and experience God in a way that changes everything!"

—BOB BEAUDINE, best-selling author of *The Power of WHO!* and *2 Chairs*

"When I heard Jarrett Stephens talk about a preaching series he was going to do on the mountaintop experiences found in the Bible, I thought it was such a great idea. So many important events in the Bible take place on a mountain: Mount Carmel, Mount Moriah, Mount Sinai, and the Mount of Transfiguration. At each venue we see that God is the protector, the provider, the sustainer, the transformer, and so much more. Let God take you to the mountaintop and experience a new point of view."

—KERBY ANDERSON, president of Probe Ministries and host of *Point of View* radio talk show

THE MOUNTAINS
ARE CALLING

Making the Climb
for a Clearer View of God
and Ourselves

JARRETT STEPHENS

Foreword by DR. JACK GRAHAM

MULTNOMAH

The Mountains Are Calling

All Scripture quotations, unless otherwise indicated, are taken from the Holy Bible, English Standard Version, ESV® Text Edition® (2016), copyright © 2001 by Crossway Bibles, a publishing ministry of Good News Publishers. All rights reserved. Scripture quotations marked (NASB) are taken from the New American Standard Bible®. Copyright © 1960, 1962, 1963, 1968, 1971, 1972, 1973, 1975, 1977, 1995 by the Lockman Foundation. Used by permission. (www.Lockman.org). Scripture quotations marked (NIV) are taken from the Holy Bible, New International Version®, NIV®. Copyright © 1973, 1978, 1984 by Biblica Inc.® Used by permission. All rights reserved worldwide.

Details in some anecdotes and stories have been changed to protect the identities of the persons involved.

Trade Paperback ISBN 978-0-7352-9119-5
eBook ISBN 978-0-7352-9120-1

Cover design by Kristopher K. Orr

Published in the United States by Multnomah, an imprint of the Crown Publishing Group, a division of Penguin Random House LLC, New York.

MULTNOMAH® and its mountain colophon are registered trademarks of Penguin Random House LLC.

Library of Congress Cataloging-in-Publication Data
Names: Stephens, Jarrett, 1978– author.
Title: The mountains are calling : making the climb for a clearer view of God and ourselves / Jarrett Stephens.
Description: First Edition. | Colorado Springs : Multnomah, 2018.
Identifiers: LCCN 2017055641| ISBN 9780735291195 (pbk.) | ISBN 9780735291201 (electronic)
Subjects: LCSH: Mountains in the Bible. | Mountains—Religious aspects—Christianity.
Classification: LCC BS630.S66 2018 | DDC 220.9/1—dc23
LC record available at https://lccn.loc.gov/2017055641

Printed in the United States of America
2018—First Edition

10 9 8 7 6 5 4 3 2 1

SPECIAL SALES
Most Multnomah books are available at special quantity discounts when purchased in bulk by corporations, organizations, and special-interest groups. Custom imprinting or excerpting can also be done to fit special needs. For information, please email specialmarketscms@penguinrandomhouse.com or call 1-800-603-7051.

*To Debbie and my girls: Riley, Kelsey,
Landry, and Cameron.*

*There is no one I would rather ascend the
mountains of life with than you.*

Those who trust in the LORD are like Mount Zion,
which cannot be moved, but abides forever.
As the mountains surround Jerusalem,
so the LORD surrounds his people,
from this time forth and forevermore.

PSALM 125:1–2

Contents

Foreword

The Christian life is a series of mountaintops and valleys, and the way up is not always a straight path or an easy road. There are many obstacles and challenges along the way. But once you reach the top, you realize the climb was worth it. At the top of the mountain is clearer air, a longer look, and the achievement of getting there. Call it perspective. Because once you have arrived, mountaintop experiences are fresh, exhilarating, and fulfilling and inspiring as well. The old hymn says: *"I'm pressing on the upward way. New heights I'm gaining every day. Still praying as I'm onward bound, 'Lord, plant my feet on higher ground.'"*

As you read Jarrett Stephens's *The Mountains Are Calling,* you will encounter God in the summit places of the Bible. So often God met his people and pointed them to a better future from the vantage point and clear perspective of a mountaintop.

Looking back on my own life, I celebrate those uplifting, elevating moments when it seems you can reach out and touch God. Every Christian should seek the summits and desire a higher plane of life. Jarrett Stephens will help take you through a journey onward and upward. As my dear friend and Prestonwood member, Zig Ziglar, used to say: "See you at the top!" For there at the top of the mountain, we experience God's best for our lives.

I can say without hesitation that Jarrett Stephens understands *the upward way.* He is a "mountaineer." From the first day I met him as a young Prestonwood intern and first-year seminary student, his upside potential was obvious. Enthusiastic, godly, gifted, hungry, sincere, and humble, Jarrett began his ministry and ascended to the highest level of leadership in our church. Now, as our teaching pastor, he proclaims God's Word and teaches Scripture in a way that is real, engaging, and yes, uplifting.

So, let me encourage you to join in on the journey with Jarrett Stephens as our guide. From Mount Moriah to Olivet, to Calvary and much more, let's climb together and breathe deeply of the rare air of spiritual heights. And then, from the mountaintops, let us shout it to all the world: *Jesus is Lord!*

Dr. Jack Graham
Pastor, Prestonwood Baptist Church

And I Must Go

The mountains are calling and I must go, and I
will work on while I can, studying incessantly.

JOHN MUIR, IN AN 1873
LETTER TO HIS SISTER

I was not familiar with the name John Muir until a friend of mine who knew I was working on this project introduced me to him and his life's work. Most people knew him as "John of the Mountains." Muir was a naturalist and wrote a number of books describing his exploits and adventures traveling through and living in the mountains.

Google search his name and this quote will appear eventually: "The mountains are calling and I must go." You can find it on everything these days from T-shirts to coffee mugs. But it is actually an abbreviated quote. What's missing from the usual quote is this: "and I will work on while I can, studying incessantly." Sure, those missing words don't make a big difference, but they do shed some light on the purpose behind Muir's mountain travels. They were not just weekend getaways but rather intentional journeys with the goal of bringing information and inspiration back to the people down below. Muir clearly felt both privilege and responsibility in relation to wonders such as Yosemite and the Sierras and refused to keep to himself what he had learned and experienced in the mountains. He was working for his generation and, whether he realized it or not, for generations to come.

Above and Beyond the Normal of Life

Let it be said, I'm no John Muir, but I do love the mountains. A few years ago I flew to Colorado to preach at a summer camp for the high school students from our church, Prestonwood Baptist Church in Plano, Texas. As a twenty-eight-year veteran of church camps, I had a pretty good understanding of the summer-camp environment. Some of you who grew up in church know this environment too. These camps provide a reprieve from the routine of life. Cell phone use is limited so there is a break from technology and the social media that so often fights for the students' attention. For a week, students learn what it means to seek after and worship the Lord without the everyday responsibilities that typically preoccupy their minds and fill their schedules.

I initially thought I'd come to the camp and use some sermons that I had in my preaching arsenal. After preaching at years of camps, I knew exactly what type of messages the students needed to hear: sermons on salvation and holiness, calling the students to revival and away from rebellious living. Why reinvent the wheel? I'd just take a few old sermons, freshen up the illustrations, and rehash them to the best of my ability.

But on this particular occasion, I couldn't shake the thought that I needed to do something new. It was as if God was letting me know that old, leftover sermons just weren't going to work, at least not that summer.

As I began to think and pray about the week, I started reading through my Bible and asked God to give me a series of messages that would really challenge and encourage the students to engage with Christ like never before. I wanted God to speak to me and speak to the students in a fresh way. After all, this was camp, and

I wanted these high schoolers to leave camp the same way I did all those years I attended as a camper. I wanted them to have a "mountaintop experience" with God.

If you have been a follower of Jesus for very long, you know what I mean by that term "mountaintop experience." It's a high mark in your walk with the Lord. You sense a closeness to him like never before. His presence is near. Your spiritual vision seems clear, and your resolve to follow him no matter what the cost is strong. It's here that personal resolutions are made and personal convictions are solidified. From a spiritual standpoint, it's as if you're on top of the world.

This is what I wanted the students to experience, and this was on my mind as I was flying over the mountains to preach at camp that summer. It was in this moment God led me to begin thinking through and reflecting on my own mountaintop experiences with him through the years. Many of them occurred at a camp just like the one where I was headed. While overlooking the mountains below, I sensed this question stirring in my heart: *Why not preach to the students about the mountaintop experiences found throughout the Scriptures?*

Now, I am not one who claims to hear the audible voice of God. I read the Bible. I pray. I enjoy listening to the preaching of God's Word and have a lot of friends who can speak godly counsel into my life. Through the years, these are the normal avenues that I have found myself "hearing from the Lord." On that airplane though, the still small voice speaking to me at thirty thousand feet seemed louder than ever. It was a word the Lord was speaking straight to my heart, and it quickly became a quest. I knew what God wanted me to do. He wanted me to take these students to the mountains of Scripture to experience him.

So I started studying the mountaintop moments in the Bible. I began reading every reference to mountains I could find and was blown away by what I discovered. I had no idea how many epic stories of faith that we read in our Old and New Testaments happened on mountains. It seemed that often when God wanted to reveal a truth, command commitment from the people, or instruct in a significant way, he would call his prophets or his people to a mountain.

- Abraham was called to sacrifice his son, Isaac, on Mount Moriah and learned there that God would provide for him and meet his needs.

- Moses not only met God in a burning bush on a mountain but was allowed into the presence of God and given the Ten Commandments on top of Mount Sinai.

- Elijah battled the prophets of Baal and found God to be an all-consuming power on Mount Carmel.

- Jesus preached his first major sermon not from the synagogue in his hometown or the temple in Jerusalem but on the side of a mountain in Galilee. He modeled intimacy with God throughout his ministry as he broke away from the crowds and went to unspecified

mountains to pray. He revealed his glory to his
disciples in the Transfiguration on Mount Hermon.
His suffering, betrayal, ascension, and eventual return
all happen on a mountain called Olivet. He gave the
church its mission statement from an unnamed
mountain in Galilee.

So many of the most important events and teachings of Scripture took place on mountaintops. I was amazed at this truth that I was personally uncovering for the first time.

When we landed in Colorado, I was ready to preach. I just had to decide which mountains I would use to show the students how God worked, how he moved on these mountaintops. The journey we walked together those days in Colorado made for an incredible summer camp.

It was fun seeing God move in the hearts of the students that week in the same way he had moved in mine through the years. It was rewarding watching as campers worshipped him with undivided hearts, enjoyed community with limited distractions, and gave their lives to Christ for the first time. Let's just say it was transformative in my own life too. Through my preaching about the mountaintop moments in Scripture, we had our own mountaintop experiences with God in the mountains of Colorado. And I have returned often to the truths we talked about that week at camp.

For a number of years, I've thought about that series of messages and what God did in my heart that summer. What made it so special? What was it about these mountains in Scripture that seemed to move me and the students to respond to God in the way that we did that week? It was a question I carried for some time.

Ironically, I finally figured out the answer to this question on another mountaintop. A few years ago my family went with some friends to Red River, New Mexico. While it's often a destination for college students during spring break, during the summer it's more tame and family friendly. We were excited about getting out of the blistering heat of Dallas and found what we were looking for in the cooler weather of the Sangre de Cristo Mountains near Taos.

Red River has a population of less than five hundred, though it swells to quite a bit more during the different seasons. Each year my girls enjoy riding a ski gondola up the mountain. They love trying to spot animals in the woods beneath us on the way up, while I nervously arm-guard them and make sure they don't fall off. On the way down, they like to look into the tiny town far below and try to find the place where we are staying or point out where we will eat ice cream later that evening. It always amazes me how different the view is from the top of the mountain. From the top, the small town looks even smaller. Nature, and by extension God, looks so much bigger. The view from the mountain puts things into perspective.

I believe the same can be said about studying these mountains in Scripture. And I think this is what made that week of camp so unique and memorable. Life comes at us pretty hard, pretty fast, and on a pretty consistent basis. But on the mountain, God gives his people a respite. When we encounter him, things change.

Simply Nothing like It

My family loves the ministry of Sky Ranch and attends the family camp they host each year in Ute Trail, Colorado. If you haven't figured it out by now, I'm a fan of camp and trying to pass this love on to my kids. For the last few years we have made our way to this camp and take great pride in being a part of what they call "Week One." You would think it would be better to go to camp later in the summer after the counselors have had some experience with other families and have gotten all the kinks worked out for camp. But we have found our niche and also some of our best friends in attending that first week. What I like most about it is that it starts the summer off, right out of the gate. The kids are out of school on Friday and we are in Colorado by Sunday.

With four girls under the age of twelve, loading up the car and taking off on the two-day, fifteen-hour drive north through Texas has its challenges. I have no idea how parents in the previous generations made it without technology. I thank God for movies and earbuds. They keep me sane on these long trips. It's always a welcome sight to see the terrain change and feel the weather getting cooler as we enter the mountains of Colorado. We absolutely love it. It may take a day or two to shift gears in our thinking, but jump-starting the summer in this way forces us to slow down and really take in the fact that vacation has begun.

There are twelve or so cabins on the campground of Ute Trail, and each family is assigned to its own. Because of the size of our family, we get the same large cabin every year. It is only a few yards away from a small pond and surrounded by mountains on every side. The setting is beautiful as the campground sits right in the middle of the Gunnison and Rio Grande National Forests. It's the perfect backdrop. There is not much better than getting up early, grabbing a cup of coffee, and watching the sun rise over the Rockies. And there, each morning, I make it a practice to spend time alone with God. I breathe in the fresh air. I take in his creation. I pray. There is simply nothing like it.

After breakfast, all the people in the camp make their way down to a little white chapel for morning worship. Situated away from everything else on the campsite, in the middle of an open field, it looks as if it could be a small schoolhouse on the set of *Little House on the Prairie*. The back of the chapel is solid glass that gives a breathtaking view of the snow-covered mountain range looming over the camp. On the walls of the chapel, ten stained-glass windows, five on each side, share the story of redemption from episodes in Scripture, and between those walls are about twenty rows of pews. My family fills an entire row every morning.

Morning worship is usually rather simple. There is one guitar, and two counselors sing familiar praise songs. And though the morning worship time is not mandatory, I don't know of anyone who misses it. I certainly don't.

A couple of years ago, on a morning like any other, I was sitting in one of these worship moments. I was surrounded by family, holding one of my youngest in my arms. I don't remember the song we were singing, but I fell silent. I became acutely aware of my unworthiness before a holy God and at the same time was overwhelmed by his love and grace for me. I didn't deserve the wife who was worshipping by my side or the children whom he had blessed us with, and yet there we all were, worshipping Jesus as a family.

In that moment, it was as if time went into slow motion and God allowed me to see his eternal purpose for my life. Everything seemed to be at peace and to be right. A mountaintop moment that I wasn't expecting or looking for.

I realize we can't manipulate God and manufacture these times with him. But there is no denying we long for them. There is something in us that desires the presence of Jesus. We want him to draw close to us and reveal more of himself to us. We want and need to experience moments with him like this. Even as I write and think about God's moving in my heart and life as encapsulated in these memories, there is a longing in me to return to those places. I want to sense the nearness of God now as I did back then.

Maybe as you read you are having this same thought. It may even be why you picked up this book. You have memories of mountaintop moments in your life and want to experience God now the way you did on the mountain.

Here's what's interesting, though. I've discovered I don't have to go back to those literal places to have mountaintop moments with God. I can experience him now, right where I am. All I have to do is open my Bible, begin reading, and invite him to speak to me through his Word.

This is one of the main reasons I made the decision to write this book. I am convinced that God loves to give us mountaintop-type experiences with him and uses these times to draw us closer to him and propel us forward in our walk with him.

Mountaintop moments, moments when we ascend into God's presence, give us a taste of his glory and, like a carrot dangling in front of a rabbit, leave us longing and aching for more. A fresh glimpse of who he is pushes us more into his presence so that we can grow in our relationship with him and help change the world around us.

On the mountain, we discover two important truths. First, *God changes our perspective of who he is.* We learn that he is not a distant God uninvolved in and unfamiliar with his created world. Instead, he is concerned with the affairs of his children. He is interested in the smallest details of our lives and cares about what we are going through. He is a God who empathizes with us and desires to walk alongside us.

The second truth we discover on the mountain is *God changes our perspective of who we are.* It's on the mountain that God reveals to us our weaknesses and insecurities. We find in our relationship with him strength we didn't know existed. We see in these moments that the world really does not revolve around us. We are given a mission and have a part to play in that mission that we could never imagine.

With a new perspective of God and a new perspective of ourselves, we walk into a new way of experiencing him. We are never the same after ascending the mountain.

This book will cover ten mountaintop moments and how the events that took place (or will take place) affect our lives today. We'll discover together how much God loved taking people to places where he could change their perspective of who he is, places where he could change their perspective of who they were.

I should issue a warning, though. Like in all mountain climbing, we're not meant to live on the mountaintops. There comes a time when we must descend the mountain. In the same way, mountaintop experiences with God are not meant to last forever. They are moments in time, and just as we ascend and get a breathtaking view, there always comes a time when we must descend the mountain as well. We are meant to take what God did in us there, take what he taught us there, and allow it to help us change the world around us.

The mountains are still calling. God is still calling. He is issuing an invitation for us to join him today, an invitation to experience him unlike ever before. Let's ascend and make the climb together. We must go.

2

Mount Moriah

The God Who Is Provider

We all have moments in our lives when an event takes place that is so significant, we forever remember exactly where we were and what we were doing at the time the event happened. For my parents' generation, it was hearing the news of the assassination of President John F. Kennedy or watching Neil Armstrong take his first steps on the moon. For me, I vividly remember sitting in a classroom in my elementary school and watching the space shuttle *Challenger* explode in midair off the coast of Cape Canaveral. And will any of us ever forget where we were when we first heard the news of the attacks on the World Trade Center and Pentagon on September 11, 2001?

In these most memorable moments, we can recall the minutest details, like whom we were with and what we were wearing. Such events are ingrained in our minds. Somehow they have a way of changing us.

Take This World

July 7, 2016, was also this kind of day for me. I was home watching television when the news interrupted with a "Breaking Now" feature. Camera footage showed downtown Dallas in what appeared to be total chaos. People screamed as they ran through the streets. Police lights flashed everywhere. Officers hid behind their police cars and waved to get people's attention, shouting at them to take cover. It was a nightmare.

It wasn't long before reports started coming in that a shooter had interrupted a protest. But no one knew who the gunman was or how many lives he had taken. The suspect was still at large, and the city was on complete lockdown. Was this a terrorist attack? No one seemed to know what was happening.

I could not look away from the television. To say that what I was watching was surreal is an understatement. How could something like this be happening in my city?

By the end of the night, the news reported this was the worst loss of life for police and public servants since 9/11. Micah Xavier Johnson, an army veteran suffering from PTSD, was upset with the recent shootings of two African American men by police officers in Minnesota and Louisiana. He was angry and mentally disturbed, and he went to this protest in Dallas heavily armed.

In an event that no one could have ever imagined, Johnson ambushed the police officers who were assigned to ensure the safety of all those involved in the protest. He opened fire on the officers who were closest to him. Michael Krol, an eight-year veteran of the Dallas Police Department, was the first of four police officers to lose their lives that day.

The days following the shooting were incredibly tough for our community, and our church wanted to serve the police department in any way possible. We opened our hearts and our church building, hosting two of the funerals for these valiant heroes. Officer Michael Krol's funeral was one of those held at our church.

My heart was broken as I met with Michael's family to plan his funeral. Michael was one of three children. He was the caretaker of the family in many ways, and I could tell they were devastated and still in a state of shock. Who wouldn't be?

My thoughts turned to the service the next day. What could I say to comfort this grieving family, Michael's coworkers and fellow officers, and our community?

The night before the funeral I still had nothing. I sat in my study at home for hours, just staring at a blank screen, asking the Lord to give me the exact words that he wanted me to communicate. Finally, at midnight I decided to go to bed, resolved to wake up early the next morning, hoping I'd have enough time to finish before the funeral actually started.

As I laid my head on my pillow, I could not seem to gather my thoughts. The pain on the faces of Michael's family and the sense of loss they were experiencing weighed heavy on my heart. Their hurt was something that I knew I could not fix with a sermon. I lay there in the dark, praying and thinking about the conversation I had earlier that evening with the family. That's when I recalled Michael's favorite song.

I remembered that Michael's sister, Aimee, told me he loved "Where I Belong." The lyrics communicate a simple but beautiful truth.

This is not where I belong;
Take this world and give me Jesus.[1]

Those words resonated in my heart, and as I thought about them, I began to craft the funeral message around the lyric: *Take this world and give me Jesus.*

The next day I preached Michael's funeral. It was attended by well over five thousand people. As I preached, I could not escape those words. The words to this song provoked in me something that I could not explain. It came in the form of conviction. Could I say with integrity that I wanted Jesus more than the things of this world? Could I say I'd sacrifice everything to get him?

In that moment, even though I was the pastor charged with this important task of spiritually leading a community through an unspeakable tragedy, I knew the deep truth that I had wrestled with in the past and continued to work through. I was looking for more intimacy in my relationship with Jesus. I just didn't know that finding it would come at such a cost, such a sacrifice.

Intimacy. Doesn't it always come at a sacrificial cost? Consider Mount Moriah and the story of Abraham and Isaac. Consider how God led Abraham to the mountain of meeting, the mountain of provision, the mountain of intimacy.

The Call to the Mountain

You may remember the story of Abraham. This Old Testament hero was still going strong at the ripe old age of seventy-five when God commanded him to leave his extended family to go to a foreign land, a land he had never seen. The book of Genesis recounts it this way:

> Now the LORD said to Abram, "Go from your country
> and your kindred and your father's house to the land that I

will show you. And I will make of you a great nation, and I will bless you and make your name great, so that you will be a blessing. I will bless those who bless you, and him who dishonors you I will curse, and in you all the families of the earth shall be blessed. (12:1–3)

Quite the command, isn't it? And like many other times in Scripture, the request from God came with a promise. He promised Abraham that he would make him into a great nation, and he used an illustration so the promise might stick.

The LORD said to Abram, after Lot had separated from him, "Lift up your eyes and look from the place where you are, northward and southward and eastward and westward, for all the land that you see I will give to you and to your offspring forever. I will make your offspring as the dust of the earth, so that if one can count the dust of the earth, your offspring also can be counted. Arise, walk through the length and the breadth of the land, for I will give it to you." (13:14–17)

Throughout Abraham's life, God constantly reassured him of this promise, that he'd have innumerable offspring.

He brought him outside and said, "Look toward heaven, and number the stars, if you are able to number them." Then he said to him, "So shall your offspring be." (15:5)

The dust of the earth? The stars in the sky? Those were incredible pictures of the incredible promise given by God to Abraham. There was only one problem, and it was a *big* one. Abraham was seventy-five years of age, and Sarah, his wife, was sixty-five at the time of this calling. And they were childless.

Take that in one more time, slowly: seventy-five and sixty-five. These are not prime childbearing ages. And at that age, who would even want a newborn? I am a thirty-nine-year-old father of four at the time of this writing. Thinking of having another now, even at my relatively young age, makes me tired. What if I were seventy-five?

If you know anything about the story of Abraham and his faith journey, you know the man to whom three major faiths look to as the "father of their faith" was by no means a perfect man. He made his fair share of mistakes.

He lied on occasions and often feared man more than God. When he first went into Egypt, fearful for his own life, he convinced the Egyptians and ultimately Pharaoh that Sarah, his wife, was really simply his sister. You would think he would have learned better after being corrected by God about this, but then he did the exact same thing just a few years later as they journeyed into the land of Gerar.

At times, Abraham ran ahead of God and didn't lead Sarah, his wife, very well. A simple reading of the account of Sarah and her conflict with Hagar leads to this conclusion. Abraham made his own plans, thinking his timing and ingenuity were better than

God's promises. This led to the birth of Ishmael, and today we are still dealing with the consequences of that decision.

But in spite of Abraham's failure, sin, or lack of faithfulness to God, God made a promise. And God always keeps his promises. When Abraham was one hundred years old, God finally gave him and Sarah the son of promise—Isaac. And with Isaac came the fulfillment of the covenant between God and Abraham, and, with that fulfillment, the blessings of God.

We don't know much about Isaac's childhood, but scholars suggest that somewhere between ten and twenty years after his birth, "God tested Abraham . . ." (22:1). Averaging it out, when Abraham was 115, God came and called him to the mountain for the most brutal of tests:

> [God] said to him, "Abraham!" And he said, "Here I am."
> He said, "Take your son, your only son Isaac, whom you
> love, and go to the land of Moriah, and offer him there as
> a burnt offering on one of the mountains of which I shall
> tell you." (verses 1–2)

In this story, God shouted Abraham's name. And Abraham responded, "Here I am, Lord!" It's a statement of surrender. It was as if Abraham was saying "I am here and at your command." Little did he know what God was about to ask.

He said, "Take your son, your only son Isaac, whom you

love, and go to the land of Moriah, and offer him there as
a burnt offering on one of the mountains of which I shall
tell you." (verse 2)

Wait, what? Take his son? Could God mean this? What about
Abraham's descendants, the ones who were promised to outnum-
ber the stars? How could that happen if . . . ? This was Abraham's
call to the mountain. Would answering it cost Abraham
everything?

The Cost of the Climb

I don't know about you, but I struggle with what God commanded and asked of Abraham. For those of us familiar with this
story, it's easy to read past it without being too empathetic because
we know how it ends. It's also easy to skip over this "small" detail
in the story because of the gruesome nature of what was being
asked. But if we take a step back and really think about this situation, it's truly a punch to the gut. It takes our breath away.

If you have children, you want to banish from your mind immediately the thought of losing one. I don't think I could imagine
anything that could cause more hurt or despair. In a very real way,
this is what Abraham was having to wrestle through. He didn't
have the luxury of knowing how this story was going to end. Isaac
was his son, his only son.

The phrase "your only son" is used three times in this passage in Genesis with an emphasis on Isaac being the child of promise. The writer of Genesis wanted us to feel Abraham's fear, his sense of impending loss, his sorrow. Can you even begin to imagine it?

In the Hebrew sacrificial system that was to come, God always required the first tenth of all that someone owned. Whether it was the firstfruits of the crops or the firstborn of the cattle, giving God the firsts represented giving God not only your best but your very life.

The sacrifice God called Abraham to make, though, involved something far beyond just one-tenth of his best. God desired for Abraham to give to him that which Abraham treasured the most: his promised son. God wanted it all—Abraham's life, his whole world—and this is what Isaac represented.

If Abraham had ears to hear it, he would have heard God saying, "I'm inviting you into intimacy with me, Abraham. You are going to know me as you have never known me before, experience me at a deeper level than you could ever imagine. But you have to be willing to trust me. You have to be willing to sacrifice everything that you have and all that you are."

There is always a cost to knowing God fully. Always.

Knowing God requires us to lay everything on the altar of sacrifice. It begins with a complete and total renunciation of our own dreams, desires, maybe even identity. Only those who are serious about their relationship with God will ascend this mountain.

The question God had for Abraham in that moment is the same question he has for me and you today: "Do you trust me? Do you want to know me? Do you treasure me above all other things? Do I have your heart?"

I love how Abraham responded:

> So Abraham rose early in the morning, saddled his
> donkey, and took two of his young men with him, and his
> son Isaac. And he cut the wood for the burnt offering and
> arose and went to the place of which God had told him.
> (Genesis 22:3)

Notice that Abraham didn't negotiate or hesitate. There's no indication of objection in Scripture, though that had to be a sleepless night. Despite what must have been great inner turmoil, Abraham made the decision to obey God at the cost of his own son.

Abraham walked by faith. He was going where God had called him to go and doing what God told him to do. Surrender. Obedience. This is how the journey to knowing God begins. And it all begins with a choice, just one step of faith. This is how Abraham made it up the mountain, and it's what will get us up the mountain.

If you want to experience and know God, it starts by surrendering your entire life to God's will and to his Word. And this isn't an easy decision or journey. If it were, every Christian would be walking in this truth. Remember, there is a cost. Always.

Like Abraham, we are faced with a choice. It's a choice that involves the mind, the heart, and the will. The temptation as we ascend this mountain is to focus on what we are giving up or what we are called to sacrifice. This will only stall our progress up the mountain. The way of wisdom is to put our focus on God and trust him one step at a time, one day at a time. It is a daily decision to walk in obedience, and by faith put one foot in front of the other. This is how we ascend the mountain to know God, even when he has called us to do the seemingly impossible.

But we can't forget the dramatic conclusion to this story. Abraham took his son up that mountain by faith and laid him on the altar just as he was commanded. This scene gets me every time I read it:

> Then Abraham reached out his hand and took the knife to slaughter his son. But the angel of the LORD called to him from heaven and said, "Abraham, Abraham!" And he said, "Here I am." He said, "Do not lay your hand on the boy or do anything to him, for now I know that you fear God, seeing you have not withheld your son, your only son, from me." (verses 10–12)

Abraham's absolute obedience stirred the heart of the God who promises and provides. And there, caught in a thicket by its horns, was a ram. There was a substitution on the mountain that day. Abraham sacrificed the ram instead of his son, his only son.

> So Abraham called the name of that place, "The LORD will provide"; as it is said to this day, "On the mount of the LORD it shall be provided." (verse 14)

Was it worth it to follow God up the mountain? Absolutely. On that mountain, Abraham came to know God in a new way. He met God the provider, the One who saved his son. Through that provision, God reaffirmed his promise of blessing to Abraham. God showed Abraham that . . .

When you have me . . .

When you lean on me . . .

When you trust in me . . .

When you walk with me . . .

When you follow me to the mountain, you will find that I am your perfect provision. My promises are all you need. My grace is sufficient.

On the mountain, God changes our perspective of who he is. There we find that he is not a demanding ruler, a god of requirements with a short fuse. He's not heartlessly putting us through tests, seeing whether he can cause us to stumble. On the mountain, we see that God provides everything we need, everything we've been looking for and desiring, namely himself. He gives us an experiential knowledge of his promises and his presence.

When we answer God's call to the mountain and learn of his provision, God changes our perspective of ourselves too. He shows us that we can climb the mountain of sacrifice knowing that he is faithful, that he will make himself known. Realizing this, we are able to say with integrity, "Take this world and give me Jesus. I'll sacrifice anything if it means knowing him more intimately."

This is what mountaintop moments are all about: knowing

God in a deeper, more personal way. And though intellectual knowledge about God can be useful, what he really wants us to discover on the mountain is an experiential knowledge. This was what God wanted to show Abraham on Mount Moriah. Abraham *knew* the promises God had made, but God wanted him to understand the promise in a real and personal way. He wanted Abraham to see him as provider.

It's Worth It

God calls us to the mountain so that we can know him in his fullness: as provider, fulfiller, and loving father. It's a call you don't want to miss out on. Anyone who has made the decision to ascend this mountain will tell you that it's worth it. In reality, it's the only thing worthy of our lives. This hit home for me the day we laid Michael Krol to rest, the day I read those lyrics: "Take this world and give me Jesus."

It's been over two years now since I preached Michael's funeral. I reflect on it from time to time, and outside of the Scripture text I preached, I don't really remember much of what I said. What I do remember is looking over a flag-draped casket to a congregation of people and being confronted with my own mortality. I resolved that day to know God, no matter the cost, and to walk up the mountain to experience him in new ways. I resolved to know him in a greater way, even if it meant sacrificing everything.

3

Mount Sinai

The God Who Is Holy

Have you ever had one of those moments in life when you sensed the very presence and weight of the glory of God? I'm not talking about getting goose bumps in a church service or worshipping during an emotional high. I'm talking about becoming face-on-the-floor overwhelmed because you are confronted with the reality of God's holiness.

Words seem pointless in times like these. It feels better and even more natural to stay silent. You become aware of how small you really are, and there is a deep realization of the waywardness of your own heart.

In God's presence, you sense how far away you are from where you need to be. At the same time, though, there is no place you would rather be. Feelings of fear or of being unworthy might be present, but at the same time, they seem to drown in the love of God, in your deep sense of awe of who he is.

These types of mountaintop moments with God can't be manufactured, but you can put yourself in a position to experience them.

Why Have I Never Done This Before?

For our one-year anniversary, my wife and I celebrated by escaping to her aunt and uncle's lake house a few hours away from Dallas. They have a beautiful home nestled in the middle of some huge pine trees on one of the most picturesque lakes in East Texas. It was quiet. It was romantic. And best of all, it was free. We had a few great days recalling all that had taken place in our first year together. From learning how to balance work, ministry, and family, to discovering different strengths and weaknesses in our character, we were grateful to be with each other and excited about the journey we were on.

When the weekend came to a close, we met some family friends for lunch. My wife traveled back to Dallas with them because I had decided beforehand to take some vacation time and have a three-day spiritual retreat of sorts. And lest you think I am superspiritual, I'd never done anything like that before and haven't since. But on this occasion I was looking forward to an extended time alone with the Lord. I made the decision that with the exception of checking in with my wife, I wouldn't watch any television, listen to any music, or use the internet. I would be alone, technology free. I also decided to fast from food for the sole purpose to intensely seek God in prayer and through reading his Word. All I had with me were a change of clothes, my Bible, my journal, and a few books to read and keep me company.

I was amazed at how long it took me to get used to the silence and was equally amazed by my inability to focus for long periods of time. I am a people person by nature and don't have to look for distractions. It took a full day and a half to calm my internal drive to do something. It was hard not feeling the rush of checking something off a list or trying to accomplish a feat or challenge of some kind. I had either forgotten how or never learned to rest, and the peace and quiet felt like strangers. I was not familiar or comfortable with any of it.

But after the first day and a half, the internal drive slowed, and I was able to begin to think clearly. I could sense that my mind and heart became freed from the tyranny of the urgent and the pressing needs and responsibilities of work. There was not a whole lot to do, and I purposely avoided any activities like exercising or fishing. I wanted to be still before the Lord—period.

In the morning, I watched the sun rise over one side of the lake and then watched it set on the other in the evening. I took several long walks down winding country roads, stopping from time to time to look out over a pasture or observe cattle grazing. I had no one to talk to but God in those moments, and I was resolved to think and dwell on nothing but him.

And something happened in those three days at the lake house. I became acutely aware of the presence of God. And there, all I could keep thinking was *Why have I never done this before?*

An Incredible Privilege

The life of Moses has always intrigued me. One of my earliest memories is of being in a Sunday school class and learning the story of Moses's deliverance from death when he was an infant. I can still see the poster-board picture of his mother lowering him into a basket and placing it in the river. That singular image set my imagination on fire.

Pharaoh's daughter discovered the baby Moses in a basket in the reeds of the Nile. Moses was raised in the palace and had all the benefits that came along with it. He was a Hebrew living in the midst of Egyptians. As he grew up, he became aware of this privilege. Later he took the life of an Egyptian man he saw beating a Hebrew slave, and ultimately that life-altering decision led to a life on the run.

Nearly forty years later, as a fugitive in the desert, Moses had an encounter with God that would change his life forever. Providentially, it took place on a mountain. You may not remember the whole story, but I bet you remember pieces of it. God spoke to Moses from a burning bush and gave him the assignment to lead the Hebrew nation out of bondage and into the Promised Land. This set Moses and the people of Israel on a journey filled with the miraculous signs of their deliverance. God's chosen people were finally free.

After 430 years of slavery, many had given up on the God of Abraham, Isaac, and Jacob. They had heard the stories passed down from their great-great-grandparents about Yahweh and his relationship with the patriarchs, but he seemed to be far away from them during their time in slavery. Though as they walked out of Egypt, they saw that God still cared for them. They witnessed the work of God firsthand. He was alive. He was present. And yet he needed to reintroduce himself to the people of Israel, to show them what a relationship with him looked like.

To do this, God invited Moses up a mountain. Many believe

this to be Mount Horeb, the same mountain where God spoke to him from the burning bush. Today this mountain is better known as Mount Sinai. It was there that God revealed to Moses the Ten Commandments and established with the people a covenant that would guide them the rest of their lives.

It was an incredible privilege to meet and interact with a personal God, but being in his presence was not something Moses or the people of Israel could take lightly. Read how the Bible describes God's presence and the warning given to them surrounding it:

> The LORD said to Moses, "Behold, I am coming to you in a thick cloud, that the people may hear when I speak with you, and may also believe you forever."
>
> When Moses told the words of the people to the LORD, the LORD said to Moses, "Go to the people and consecrate them today and tomorrow, and let them wash their garments and be ready for the third day. For on the third day the LORD will come down on Mount Sinai in the sight of all the people. And you shall set limits for the people all around, saying, 'Take care not to go up into the mountain or touch the edge of it. Whoever touches the mountain shall be put to death.'" (Exodus 19:9–12)

The presence of God was everything to the people of Israel. When they were being delivered from Egypt, it was the presence of God that led them in a pillar of cloud by day and a pillar of fire by night. When God gave them instructions on how to build the tabernacle, he included specific details regarding the Most Holy Place, where the Ark of the Covenant would reside. The ark represented the dwelling place of God. He taught them how to tend to his presence and how to carry his ark before them wherever they went, even in battle.

What was it God was teaching them on the mountain about his presence? What lesson was God seeking to get across to them in the thick cloud?

The Character of God

God delivered instructions for the people, and by them, he taught the descendants of Abraham that his very presence is *infinitely holy.* No one and nothing can compare to God. In his holiness, he is completely set apart. This raises the question: Set apart from whom? From us.

God is utterly and totally different from us. There really isn't even a good illustration that could demonstrate the disparity that exists between our unrighteousness and the holiness of God. He is in a category of his own. Perfectly pure. Perfectly righteous. There is nothing in him that is dark, evil, or sinful. Not even a hint of impurity can be found in the character of God.

His presence also demonstrated that he is *full of glory.* This is what the clouds surrounding the mountain represented. "Mount

Sinai was wrapped in smoke . . . , and the whole mountain trembled greatly" (Exodus 19:18). God is so glorious that even the mountain quaked and shook in his presence.

The glory of God is a theme found throughout the Bible. Isaiah the prophet got a glimpse of God on his throne and reported that angels surround the presence of God, with a song on repeat:

> In the year that King Uzziah died I saw the LORD sitting
> upon a throne, high and lifted up; and the train of his robe
> filled the temple. Above him stood the seraphim. Each had
> six wings: with two he covered his face, and with two he
> covered his feet, and with two he flew. And one called to
> another and said:

> "Holy, holy, holy is the LORD of hosts;
>   the whole earth is full of his glory!" (Isaiah 6:1–3)

The Hebrew word for "glory" used in Isaiah is the word *kavod*. It's related to a word that means "weight or heaviness."

It was this aspect of God's character that caused the seraphim in heaven to cover their eyes in the presence of the God. No one can see the fullness of the glory of God and live. But we can see glimpses of his glory. The Bible tells us the "whole earth is full of his glory."

When I was watching those sunrises and sunsets on the lake and taking in God's creation while staring out over a moonlit pasture, I received glimpses of the glory of God. If you have ever stood at the base of a majestic mountain, stared into a starry sky, or been there for the birth of a child, you've seen a glimpse of the glory of God. All you have to do is glance in the mirror and you are seeing a glimpse of the glory of God.

What a privilege to be invited into the presence of such a glorious God. So why aren't more of us craving his presence? Why don't we do whatever it takes to be in the presence of this God who is infinitely holy and full of glory?

Suppress, Exchange, Ignore

One clear reason is that we do our best to *suppress its reality.* Simply put, this is the essence of sin. Our sin nature is an animal unto itself, and it will do anything to prevent or inhibit us from seeing, noticing, realizing, and experiencing the glory of God. Paul put it this way in the book of Romans:

> The wrath of God is revealed from heaven against all ungodliness and unrighteousness of men, who by their unrighteousness suppress the truth. For what can be known about God is plain to them, because God has shown it to them. For his invisible attributes, namely, his eternal power and divine nature, have been clearly perceived, ever since the creation of the world, in the things that have been made. So they are without excuse. (1:18–20)

Consider the ways you justify your own sin, the ways you rationalize, the ways you suppress the truth. Aren't there times when you'll do anything to avoid being confronted by the reality of God's presence? His holiness and glory have a way of putting us in our place, of showing us the darkness of our own hearts. And the truth is we don't like it.

We don't want to see the holiness of God because it brings to light the filth of our sin. And who wants to feel bad about themselves? Who wants their self-esteem to be kept in check? We don't want to come to grips with the depths of our own sin.

And even when we don't fully suppress this truth, we so often *exchange it for something else.* Paul continued in this passage in Romans:

> Although they knew God, they did not honor him as God
> or give thanks to him, but they became futile in their
> thinking, and their foolish hearts were darkened. Claim-
> ing to be wise, they became fools, and exchanged the glory
> of the immortal God for images resembling mortal man
> and birds and animals and creeping things. (verses 21–23)

Don't miss the very clear progression here. It all begins with refusing to honor God. Not honoring God leads to a place of arrogance and ingratitude. And the further we stray in our arrogance, the more our thoughts become dulled and our hearts darkened. We then find ourselves exchanging the glory of God for so many things.

I loved watching game shows as a kid. I thought it would be cool if I ever got my name called to "Come on down!" on *The Price Is Right*. If I ever did make it on the show, I guarantee I would bid a dollar no matter what product they were pushing! I also enjoyed watching *Family Feud*. Just imagine yourself in the fast-money round of *Family Feud*, and you've twenty seconds to guess the top three responses to "Things We Exchange the Glory of God For." You give your answers, and then the host comes back with "Survey says . . ."

1. The pleasures of the flesh. This is why pornography is so rampant. Sexual immorality and promiscuity may make us feel safe, loved, looked after, and in control, but in the end they leave us feeling more guilty, broken, and demeaned.

2. The pursuit of success. Success is the choice drug of so many people today. It's what we run after thinking that once we find it, then we will have arrived. In an article produced by *Fast Company,* Harriet Rubin wrote: "Of all the subjects we obsess about . . . success is the one we lie about most—that success and its cousin money will make us secure, that success and its cousin power will make us important, that success and its cousin fame will make us happy. It's time to tell the truth. . . . People are . . . using all of their means to get money, power, and glory—and then

self-destructing."[2] Self-destructing could not describe better this unhealthy exchange.

3. The approval of man. We don't say no because of a fear of letting someone else down. The result here is we find ourselves stretched too far and too thin, sacrificing time with vital relationships in order to please someone whom we may not even know. Much of what is behind our social media craze is an unhealthy and self-destructive exchange of the glory of God with the obsession of the approval of man. We obsess over what people think of us and run after what we feel will give us a sense of worth, all the while headed down a dead-end road.

Unfortunately, this is not a television game show but the way we live our everyday lives.

I'm reminded of the often-quoted Christian philosopher and apologist C. S. Lewis, who wrote in his essay "The Weight of Glory,"

It would seem that Our Lord finds our desires not too strong, but too weak. We are half-hearted creatures, fooling about with drink and sex and ambition when infinite joy is offered us, like an ignorant child who wants to go on making mud pies in a slum because he cannot imagine what is meant by the offer of a holiday at the sea. We are far too easily pleased.[3]

How tragic that we replace the infinite joy, peace, and security found in the presence of God with things that are temporary, destructive to our souls, and ultimately lead to death.

And as tragic as it may be that we suppress the glory of God or exchange the truth of God for a lie, consider that there might be something even more tragic. Many believers simply *ignore* God's presence.

Preparation—this was what was behind the command to the Israelites to consecrate themselves and wash their garments. The Lord of the universe wanted them to take the weight of his glory seriously. He wanted to guard the people from ignoring him or presuming upon his presence.

The list of those people in the Bible who suffered the severest of consequences because they neglected or ignored the rules for entering into God's presence is long and epic. In the Old Testament, each infraction, even those that were accidental, led to death.

In Leviticus 10, the sons of Aaron the high priest offered "unauthorized fire" before the Lord, and the fire came out and consumed them. In Numbers 16, a man named Korah and his followers attempted to take charge of Israel and overthrow Moses's and Aaron's leadership. They did this without the permission of God, and after they offered incense to him, the earth swallowed them whole. When the Ark of the Covenant returned to Jerusalem after being in the hands of the Philistines, the people celebrated, and the oxen transporting the ark stumbled. A man named Uzzah reached out his hand to simply steady the ark and was "struck . . . down there because of his error, and he died there beside the ark of God" (2 Samuel 6:5–7). Even in the New Testament, Ananias and Sapphira fell to a premature death because they ignored the reality of God's holiness and did not take the presence of God seriously.

What is the takeaway for us in all this? We should not enter casually into or take for granted the presence of God. There are consequences for stiff-arming his glory and avoiding his holiness. When did we begin to think that we can enter God's presence on our own terms? In fact, this was the first lesson God taught Moses when he spoke from the burning bush, when he commanded him to take off his sandals because he was standing on holy ground. The specificity regarding the sacrificial system pointed to the seriousness of the presence of God. No one could just enter the Most Holy Place and even the High Priest could only do so once a year.

I read of these encounters with God, and I consider my own life. Am I treating the presence of God with a flippant attitude? Do I need to repent for suppressing, exchanging for something lesser, or ignoring the living God? Am I ascending the mountain with great reverence, hoping to see his glory? Are you? Think about the way you enter into the presence of God. When you open your Bible to hear from him and to spend time alone with him, is there a full realization that you are walking into the Most Holy Place? When you enter into a church and people are gathered in Jesus's name to worship him, have you prepared your heart to experience the living God?

Uh-Oh

When my twins were little, one of the first words they learned was *"uh-oh."* The little sinners would sit in their high chairs and intentionally drop their bottles on the floor. Looking Mom and Dad straight in the eyes, they would then say to us, "Uh-oh." They were expressing alarm. They'd dropped something (even if intentionally), and they wanted to make us aware of it.

"Uh-oh" is often my response when I realize I am in the presence of God. Because there I realize how deeply flawed and sinful I am. I feel like it's a mistake for me to experience his greatness and glory, his presence. Naturally, I want to run the other way. Why?

When I was young in my faith, it was easy to become discouraged in my walk with Christ. It seemed the closer I would get to God, the more ungodly and unholy I would feel. It wasn't until years later that a more mature believer came alongside me and taught me that what I was experiencing was normal. Just as getting closer to a fire will make you feel more and more hot, getting closer to God will reveal more and more of our sin.

The key is to see victory in this, to understand that an increasing awareness of our lack of holiness means we are growing spiritually. So in these moments, we press on and pursue the presence of God rather than suppress, exchange, or ignore it. And how do we pursue it? We follow the same prescription God gave the people of Israel at Mount Sinai. We consecrate ourselves.

When Moses told the words of the people to the LORD,
the LORD said to Moses, "Go to the people and consecrate
them today and tomorrow." (Exodus 19:9–10)

To be in the presence of God, we must be made holy. And no amount of striving or behavior modification can make us holy. Only God can do this. Only he can consecrate us. What is consecration, though? Consecration means to be set apart. We are to be set apart positionally. God had already set apart the nation of Israel. They were his chosen people. But what does consecration mean for the modern Christian?

The Christian is set apart because of a personal relationship with God through his Son, Jesus Christ. We trust in his death, burial, and resurrection for the forgiveness of sin and to be made right with God. When we do this, we are consecrated by God and made holy.

God consecrates us from a positional standpoint, but we have the responsibility to consecrate ourselves practically. We do this by cooperating with the work of the Holy Spirit (the presence of God within us) in our life as he makes us more like Jesus. The presence of God was coming to Mount Sinai, and the people had to be prepared. They were to be consecrated. It took preparation and precaution to meet with God.

When we have been consecrated and are prepared to meet with God, we'd better be ready to encounter him in a way like never before.

Read what the people of Israel experienced when they did all God required of them:

On the morning of the third day there were thunders and lightnings and a thick cloud on the mountain and a very loud trumpet blast, so that all the people in the camp trembled. Then Moses brought the people out of the camp to meet God, and they took their stand at the foot of the mountain. Now Mount Sinai was wrapped in smoke because the LORD had descended on it in fire. The smoke of it went up like the smoke of a kiln, and the whole mountain trembled greatly. And as the sound of the trumpet grew louder and louder, Moses spoke, and God answered him in thunder. The LORD came down on Mount Sinai, to the top of the mountain. And the LORD called Moses to the top of the mountain, and Moses went up. (verses 16–20)

Talk about a mountaintop moment! God descends in fire. The very mountain trembles. From Mount Sinai God showed Israel how holy he was. Israel saw from the foot of the mountain how unholy they were. Limits had to be set; parameters had to be issued. There was no casual interchange between God and man.

The gift that God gives for meeting him on the mountain is huge. He revealed himself and ultimately gave Moses and the nation of Israel the Ten Commandments from this mountain. From that point on, the relationship between God and the nation of Israel was never the same.

Changed

Those three days alone at the lake house and in the presence of God changed me. I don't know how to express it and to this day can't describe the intimacy I experienced when I gave myself some margin and made meeting with God a priority. I have some notes written in my journal from then and return to them often, but words don't describe being in his presence.

Deep down we all desire a Mount Sinai moment. We long to be in God's presence and hear clearly from him. I'm grateful that we don't have to go to a physical mountain as Moses did to encounter God. And you don't have to go to a lake house and fast for three days as I did either. All we have to do to meet with him is to prepare our hearts, open up his Word, and wait. Because just as in Moses's and the people of Israel's case, as we prepare to go up, God is preparing to come down. And we'll never be the same.

Mount Carmel

The God Who Is Trustworthy

At nineteen I decided I couldn't hide my secret any longer. It was time to tell my parents that dark thing I'd been keeping to myself since I was eight years old. I had never shared it with anyone and thought that I would carry it with me to the grave. But some secrets grow too heavy to carry. At some point, you have to lay them down.

What my parents had assumed was an ordinary childhood was anything but ordinary. As I was growing up, much of my life revolved around the sports that my brother, sister, and I played. My mom and dad were extremely involved in our lives. I don't know how they did it, but I can't remember them ever missing a game. Up until middle school, my dad coached most of the teams we played on.

Sometimes, though, because of how the seasons were scheduled, my dad had to make a decision about which team he would coach: mine or my brother's. When it was my older brother's teams he chose to coach, I'd join a team with the rest of my friends, and we'd draw a different coach.

The summer after my first-grade year, my friends and I had a new coach. Other than my dad, he was the coach you wanted to play for. He was a winning coach, often leading his teams to the championship and then on to the all-stars. He had a reputation for coaching to win. You were considered lucky if you were a part of his team. He was the fun coach. He was popular with the kids. He wasn't married, so he would often have his players over to his house to play cards or watch movies that our parents wouldn't normally let us watch. He also owned a lake house, so swimming and water-skiing were always a part of those visits. For a kid in elementary school, it didn't get much better.

Not All Fun and Games

But things were not as they appeared at the coach's house. In the evening, after everyone went to bed, things would take a turn for the worse. He would sexually abuse me while the others slept. For four years, the abuse continued.

I never told anyone. I don't know why. Part of me was scared. In my young mind, I thought that if I told my parents, my dad would kill him. Then my dad would go to jail and I'd never see him again. Another part of me wondered whether anyone would believe me. I was also embarrassed, maybe ashamed. I chose to remain silent and say nothing through the years—that is, until I was nineteen.

I was home for the summer, working at my home church. One day I was driving to work on a two-way street. Coming in the opposite direction was my coach's familiar white Ford Bronco. I knew who was driving it as soon as I saw it. As our cars neared each other, I could see inside as it passed by me. Coach was driving, and there were two elementary schoolchildren riding with him. And I knew in that moment something had to be done.

I had always told myself that if another kid would come forward and admit to being abused, I would affirm it with the hope of locking this man up and throwing away the key. But no one ever came forward. In that moment, I knew it was up to me. I had to step forward.

Telling someone what happened to me as a child was one of the best and worst days of my life. I remember it as if it was yesterday. I'd told my youth minister the day before, and he counseled me to tell my parents. With him along for moral support, I sat with my parents after a Wednesday night church service and told them everything. My mom was devastated and sobbed, crying, "My boy! My boy!" while she hugged me. My dad stared off into space, processing his hurt, disgust, and anger.

They blamed themselves for what happened, wondering how they could have allowed this to take place. I tried as best I could to encourage them. At that point in my life, my walk with God was strong. I was studying to be in ministry and for the most part had come to terms with that part of my past. But seeing my parents' grief and shame made it one of the worst days of my life.

I say it was one of the best days of my life, though, because for the first time since I was twelve years old, I felt free. The weight I'd been carrying all those years lifted. To this day that was the best night's sleep that I can ever remember. My secret was out, and I sensed a very real nearness of the presence of God. It was a moment of brokenness, but I felt God was inviting me to a new mountain of some sort. And though I had no idea how, this would be a place where he would display his power through me.

The idea of God meeting us in our weakness to display his power is a recurring theme in Scripture. Consider the life of Elijah.

Average Elijah

The Bible does not tell us much about the background of the prophet Elijah. What we do know paints a vivid picture, though. He was a country boy, hailing from Tishbe in Gilead, a town so small that scholars are not even sure of its exact location. It was likely a backwoods village of no significance. In other words, Elijah was from the backside of nowhere.

In Elijah, God chose a man with no formal education. He was not from a family that was well off or highly respected. He was not supertalented or übergifted. The Bible goes to great lengths to communicate that he was a normal person "with a nature like ours" (James 5:17). But despite Elijah's seeming insignificance, despite his roughness around the edges, his life serves as a perfect example of God demonstrating his power through weakness.

Consider this. The God of the universe. The One who throws the stars in the heavens and knows them by name. The One who knit us together in our mothers' wombs and knew the number of our days before one of them came to be. The One who simply speaks and brings the world into existence This God demonstrates his power in and through normal, regular, average, everyday kinds of people.

There is only one catch: before God used Elijah in a big way, he first led Elijah through a period of brokenness. God brought Elijah through the valley before inviting him up the mountain.

In the Old Testament, names carried special significance and often had symbolic meanings. Elijah was born in a season in Israel's history when God's people were routinely worshipping false gods, and his name means "My God is the LORD" or "Jehovah is LORD!" Elijah's name declares his mission. This country boy would teach the people of Israel that there is only one true God.

But before Elijah's big assignment, before the call to the mountain, God invited him to a place called Cherith.

> The word of the LORD came to him: "Depart from here
> and turn eastward and hide yourself by the brook Cherith,
> which is east of the Jordan. You shall drink from the brook,
> and I have commanded the ravens to feed you there." So he
> went and did according to the word of the LORD. He went
> and lived by the brook Cherith that is east of the Jordan.
> (1 Kings 17:2–5)

In the Hebrew language *Cherith* literally means "to cut off or to cut down." The imagery is that of a tree being chopped down at its base, and this is what God was doing with Elijah during his time at Cherith. God wanted to eliminate Elijah's pride and self-reliance. Like cutting down a tall tree, God humbled Elijah so that he could then use him in a mighty and powerful way.

In Elijah's Cherith season, he had to depend on ravens to feed him in the morning and in the evening. He learned to trust God and discovered what dependence on God really looked like. God isolated Elijah. And God brought him to a point where he realized that God was all he had and God was all he needed. God was molding Elijah for something great, something purposeful, and had his undivided attention during this time.

Consider for a moment the monotony of Elijah's life. He was doing the same thing every day. All he had was his relationship with God and occasionally his raven friends. We don't know exactly how long Elijah was at Cherith. All we are told is that he was there until the brook dried up. God then commanded him to travel to another place.

> Then the word of the LORD came to him, "Arise, go to Zarephath, which belongs to Sidon, and dwell there. Behold, I have commanded a widow there to feed you." So he arose and went to Zarephath. (verses 8–10)

Another place with a name of significance, *Zarephath* comes from a word that means "to melt or to smelt." Elijah went from being cut down to being melted. Lucky guy. In Zarephath, Elijah was tested and refined. There, instead of ravens, Elijah relied on a widow to house and feed him. At Zarephath, he endured heartache and tragedy in the midst of the climax of a three-year drought. But he was an easy target, and at one point the widow blamed him for her son's death:

> After this the son of the woman, the mistress of the house, became ill. And his illness was so severe that there was no breath left in him. And she said to Elijah, "What have you

against me, O man of God? You have come to me to bring my sin to remembrance and to cause the death of my son!" (verses 17–18)

First Cherith. Then Zarephath. Would this dark season ever end? Miraculously, he brought the widow's son back to life, and this would be a lesson that he would take with him to Mount Carmel: when we are in the fire, we can be sure the God of fire is right there with us.

The Task at Hand

After long days of humbling, of smelting, of ordinariness and monotony, Elijah was eventually given quite a task. God came to him with a message for King Ahab. God was fed up with the idolatry and wickedness of Israel, and as a result of their rebellion and disobedience, a confrontation was about to take place.

To set a little background, King Solomon died. And after his death Israel entered into a prolonged civil war that divided the nation into two kingdoms, Israel to the north and Judah to the south. The southern kingdom of Judah would have twenty different kings reign throughout its history. Fewer than half are described as seeking God and doing any good at all.

The northern kingdom of Israel would not be even that lucky. Out of the nineteen kings who ruled during this time, none of them are described as good or followers of God. And Ahab was one of the worst. Scripture records, "Ahab son of Omri did more evil in the eyes of the LORD than any of those before him" (1 Kings 16:30, NIV). This is really saying something, considering Israel had experienced sixty years of murder, idolatry, and assassinations in the monarchy.

There was no one more evil than Ahab, with the possible exception of his wife, Jezebel. At one point during their reign, she gathered together as many prophets of God as she could and had them murdered. These two were known for stirring God to anger throughout their reign. As the author of 1 Kings wrote,

> As if it had been a light thing for him to walk in the sins
> of Jeroboam the son of Nebat, he took for his wife Jezebel
> the daughter of Ethbaal king of the Sidonians, and went
> and served Baal and worshiped him. . . . Ahab did more
> to provoke the LORD, the God of Israel, to anger than all
> the kings of Israel who were before him. (16:31, 33)

The king whom God told Elijah to confront was the very definition of evil. To say that the job of delivering this message would not be easy is an understatement.

How on earth would Elijah have the courage to do what God was telling him to do? Where would he find the strength to call Ahab out for his sin and disobedience? Once he did call Ahab out, wouldn't Elijah become the number one enemy of the state?

But remember, Elijah had weathered the seasons of Cherith and Zarephath. Now it was time to ascend the mountain. Elijah chose to obey God. He confronted Ahab during the third year of the drought. He called the evil king out and issued a challenge to the people of Israel.

> Elijah came near to all the people and said, "How long will you go limping between two different opinions? If the LORD is God, follow him; but if Baal, then follow him." And the people did not answer him a word. (18:21)

The word *limp* means "to waver." King Ahab was leading the people of Israel away from God. Elijah, serving as God's spokesman, made them aware that God had tolerated this for long enough. It was time for the people to make a decision. Either follow God or follow Baal. There could be no "straddling of the fence." And to help them in their decision, Elijah came up with this idea.

> "Let two bulls be given to us, and let them choose one bull for themselves and cut it in pieces and lay it on the wood, but put no fire to it. And I will prepare the other bull and lay it on the wood and put no fire to it. And you call upon the name of your god, and I will call upon the name of the LORD, and the God who answers by fire, he is God." And all the people answered, "It is well spoken." (verses 23–24)

We are told the false prophets of Baal prepared their sacrifice, and for hours, from morning until evening, they called on their god. They ranted. They raved. They cut themselves. But their God never answered. Not a single word.

Then it was Elijah's turn to prepare his sacrifice. He repaired the broken altar and poured twelve barrels of water on top of it, completely soaking the sacrifice and filling a trench around the altar. The message he wanted to send was clear. Nothing could prevent the one true God from answering by fire, not even an altar saturated with water and a sacrifice that was sopping wet. Elijah prayed,

> "Answer me, O Lord, answer me, that this people may know that you, O Lord, are God, and that you have turned their hearts back." Then the fire of the Lord fell and consumed the burnt offering and the wood and the stones and the dust, and licked up the water that was in the trench. And when all the people saw it, they fell on their faces and said, "The Lord, he is God; the Lord, he is God." (verses 37–39)

Fire fell on Mount Carmel that day, and God showed the magnitude of his power. And he demonstrated that power through a very ordinary, humbled, and melted man.

I've been to Israel a number of times, and it's always a highlight to take the groups that travel with me to the top of Mount Carmel and teach this story. We sit under a statue of Elijah erected to memorialize this event. It's something else to be on this mountain reading what happened here. It's a story that needs to be told over and over because we need to be reminded that God brings us to the mountain to demonstrate his power through ordinary and very broken people. In other words, people like us.

Refining Time

If there's one thing we learn from the life of Elijah, it's that mountaintop experiences are often preceded by days of being cut down, or weeks of melting, being in the fire.

Whenever I perform a wedding, when it is time for the exchanging of the rings, I often comment how the rings are made of the finest and purest of metals, which represents the finest and purest love the couple has for each other. The finest and purest of metals, though, must first go through a smelting process. To become pure, it must endure the heat and go through the fire. What's true for metals is true for those whom God uses.

Elijah went through his refining in Cherith and in Zarephath. God knows that trials and tough times have a way of purifying our faith and solidifying our trust in him. This is why he led Elijah through pain and suffering and why we go through pain and suffering today. The apostle Peter put it this way:

> In this you rejoice, though now for a little while, if
> necessary, you have been grieved by various trials, so that
> the tested genuineness of your faith—more precious than
> gold that perishes though it is tested by fire—may be
> found to result in praise and glory and honor at the
> revelation of Jesus Christ. (1 Peter 1:6–7)

Elijah saw the all-consuming power of God clearly displayed on Mount Carmel, but first he had to understand the faithfulness of God and learn to trust him in the midst of very difficult times. Then and only then could he see himself for who he truly was. And God for who he truly is.

The Rest of the Story

That evening when I told my parents about my coach's abuse, I could have never imagined the ways God was going to use what I went through as a child to impact people and help further his kingdom. I had no idea.

My goal was to tell what happened, hopefully protect others, and move on. What I found, though, was that God was taking me through a process of trusting him. Because the man who abused me was still coaching children, we took my news to the authorities. I made a deal with God that this was too big of a situation for me to handle by myself. I would take whatever advice or counsel was given by those who loved me. Whatever direction they led in, I would consider it as the next step in God's leading. I was ready to testify and go to court if that's what was called for. I knew justice needed to take place, and over the course of the next year, it did. Because of my testimony and coming forward, another person had the courage to go to the police and admit that he was also abused. Ultimately, my former coach was sentenced to prison and, thankfully, will never be able to coach or be around children again.

I have now been able to share my story countless times in a number of settings: churches, camps, college campuses, and advocacy centers. And every time I share it, people have come up to me afterward. They express that they experienced the same thing as a child and could never bring themselves to tell anyone. What they hear from me gives them courage and hope. Simply by sharing it with me, they find freedom, just as I did that night as a nineteen-year-old when I told my parents for the first time.

It is truly amazing. I can't get over God taking an ordinary man like me and using my story to help people find freedom, forgiveness, and the hope of a brighter future. This is God's power coming through my brokenness.

If you find yourself in a season of humbling or going through the fire of hard times, take heart. Remember Elijah and the lesson of Mount Carmel. God might be bringing you to the end of yourself. He might be breaking you in preparation for your own mountaintop experience with him, an experience in which he demonstrates his power through you. Keep trusting him, for he is trustworthy. And keep looking up, because it's only a matter of time before the fire falls.

Mount Desolate

The God Who Is Intimate

Routine. This word is sacred to me. It hasn't always been this way, but when you have four girls and have to get them all ready and out the door on time for school, routine can almost mean the difference between life and death.

All parents of young children know this to be true. There are so many variables that can throw a wrench in the routine that keeps chaos at bay. Keep the kids up too late, get them out of their routine, and prepare to pay the price in the morning. Feed them too much sugar or have them miss their afternoon nap, and rest assured, a breakdown's coming. Ship them off to the grandparents for a weekend, and prepare to retrain them on everything you have taught them up to that point.

The Hard Way

My wife and I learned this lesson the hard way when Riley, our first child, was born. We named her Riley because I felt that's what would sound the best when her name was called over the loudspeakers when she earned all-state honors in soccer one day. She had me wrapped around her finger from day one.

Debbie and I were pretty religious about her schedule. I swaddled her at the same time every night (I could swaddle like you wouldn't believe) and gave her one of the endless array of pacifiers always within reach. We fed her at the same time and put her to sleep at the same time. We could have won an award for implementing the principles found in the parental survival manuals.

We thought our parenting skills were off the charts and that Riley was the perfect baby—that is, until we decided to go eat late one night when she was around two years of age. We had been traveling that day and were making good time, so we continued to put dinner off until we arrived at our destination. We figured that before heading to check in to our hotel, we could go into a local restaurant and grab a bite to eat before turning in for the evening.

The restaurant was packed, and it took some time to get a table. We weren't worried because as award-winning parents we had snacks, Riley's favorite stuffed animal, and her blanket. We were prepared. But then something happened. As we sat down to order, our precious baby turned into a monster. She was upset. Angry. And she let the entire restaurant know about it.

We could not get her settled down. And if you've ever been in a situation like this, you know how it gets really hot, really fast. We could feel all the eyes in the restaurant looking our way. We handed Riley her stuffed animal, and she threw it on the ground. We tried to give her a pacifier, and she screamed all the louder. We knew it was bad when the manager of the restaurant came to ask whether there was anything he could do to help. To say we were embarrassed was an understatement.

Having lost control of the situation, I decided to reason with her. So I took her into the restroom and tried to convince her that her attitude and temper were not okay. Come to find out, logic doesn't work on two-year-olds.

We learned a valuable lesson that evening, one we have never forgotten: Routine matters. It matters in raising our children. It matters as it relates to our diet and physical exercise. And it matters in our spiritual formation.

Practice Makes Perfect

I love watching world-class athletes perform, and no matter the sport being played, most athletes warm up before games. They have routines. Stephen Curry dribbles multiple balls at one time and takes shots from half court before his games. Odell Beckham Jr. makes one-handed catches. All these players have routines that are sacred to them. They know the truth of the saying "Practice makes perfect," and their routines are part of their practice.

The same was true for Jesus. He had his own routine, his own version of practice making perfect. Jesus got away on a consistent basis to pray and reflect. Shortly after Jesus began his earthly ministry, Mark's gospel records:

> Rising very early in the morning, while it was still dark, he
> departed and went out to a desolate place, and there he
> prayed. (Mark 1:35)

Jesus's retreat to private prayer and reflection is one of the consistent themes we find in Luke's gospel as well. He gives four instances in the life of Jesus to show how this was a routine for him. Oftentimes after he performed miracles, large crowds would surround him, but Jesus would break away and find a private place of devotion. Consider this passage:

> Now even more the report about him went abroad, and great crowds gathered to hear him and to be healed of their infirmities. But he would withdraw to desolate places and pray. (Luke 5:15–16)

There is no doubt that some of these desolate places were mountains. Jesus loved going up to higher ground and praying. He did this before choosing his disciples:

> In these days he went out to the mountain to pray, and all night he continued in prayer to God. (6:12)

He prayed on a mountain before Peter's great confession of faith and before he walked on water. He went up to a mountain to pray with his inner circle of disciples before he was transfigured before them. He went up to "a certain place," to a mountain, and his disciples saw him, followed him, and asked him to teach them how to pray.

Breaking away from people and getting alone to pray was a regular practice for Jesus. It was his routine. And often when he went to pray alone, he made his way up a mountain.

When I read of Jesus's mountain retreats, how he got alone to be with his Father, conviction rises in my heart. If Jesus needed this, how much more do I? If Jesus made the choice to be apart from the crowds and disciples to spend time with his Father, shouldn't I do the same? Don't I need this uninterrupted time with God?

A Timely Find

Outside of the Bible, the book that has had more of a profound influence in my life than any other was one written by Aiden Wilson Tozer. I first discovered his book *The Pursuit of God* as a twenty-two-year-old seminary student. Tozer was a pastor in the Christian and Missionary Alliance movement, and in one train ride from Chicago to Dallas, he penned this book that is regarded to this day as a classic in Christian literature.

I had just graduated from a small Baptist university in Arkansas with a degree in biblical studies and had enrolled in seminary to work on a master of divinity degree. Truth be told, though, I was burned out on theology.

I was a living case study in knowing about God without knowing God.

I could write the exegetical research papers.

I could pass the theological tests (on most occasions).

I could draw a map of Israel, recount the kings and prophets in the Old Testament, and trace the missionary journeys of the apostle Paul.

I knew all about God and his people.

And yet, I was dry.

My intellectual understanding of God was robust, but my heart was cold toward the things that were important to God. I knew all about him, but I'm not sure I really knew him. I certainly was not walking intimately with him.

One day, I went into my study and looked at all the books that filled my bookshelves. And for some reason a small book caught my eye: *The Pursuit of God.* Some might call it coincidence, but I call it a life-saving moment. I pulled the book from my shelf, not knowing anything about it or its author. What I read in the introduction, though, captured my attention, and I could not put the book down. Tozer put precise words to what I was feeling.

> The Bible is not an end in itself, but a means to bring men
> to an intimate and satisfying knowledge of God, that they
> may enter into Him, that they may delight in His Presence,
> may taste and know the inner sweetness of the very God
> himself in the core and center of their hearts.[4]

Experiencing an *intimate and satisfying knowledge of God,* learning to *delight in his Presence*—these subjects felt foreign to me. I was familiar with biblical heroes like David and the apostle Paul, men with a burning desire to know God experientially.

David wrote of thirsting for God as a deer thirsts for water.

Paul wrote that he wanted to "know [Jesus] and the power of his resurrection." The word "know" that Paul chose to use is a word used in Scripture to describe the physical union between a husband and his wife. It's a different word than the common Greek word for "know" that typically points toward factual knowledge or gained insight. Like David, Paul wanted to know Christ at the deepest and most core level of his being. And this is the intimacy of relationship God desires to have with all of us.

Slowly, as I read Tozer and dove headfirst into Scripture, I was beginning to experience a true hunger for God, one that religious activity wouldn't satisfy. Yet at the same time I felt a battle happening in my soul. As much as I wanted this hunger and thirst for God, there was a real enemy trying everything in his power to prevent me from going to the mountain to pray and spend time with God. I had to figure this out.

I journaled. I prayed. I reflected on what was preventing me from taking steps toward intimacy with God, from ascending the mountain to know him in prayer. And that's when I began to recognize what I've come to call "enemies of intimacy." Over the years, I've learned they are insistent but quite predictable.

The Enemies of Intimacy

The *Merriam-Webster Dictionary* defines *enemy* as "one that is antagonistic to another; *especially:* one seeking to injure, overthrow, or confound an opponent."

Enemy #1—Busyness

As I began to practice the presence of God, it didn't take long to discover that busyness was keeping me from intimacy with God. I began to take a deeper look at my schedule, and it was no wonder that I was not satisfied spiritually. I was busy writing papers for seminary, serving on staff at my church, and dating my future wife. I wasn't getting sleep, much less slowing down to consider how shallow my walk with Christ had become.

I'd not been longing for and walking in intimacy with God because I had so many other things going on. I was burning the proverbial candle at both ends, and I was on the verge of burnout. Busyness was catching up with me, and all the activity was not adding to my spiritual life. It was draining me.

And this busyness didn't stop once I graduated from seminary. I started working full-time at the church, and it kept on keeping on. That's what busyness does. Surely you know this too? From the normal day-to-day responsibilities of attending school or raising a family to the ongoing demands of a job, don't you feel sometimes like you are constantly on a treadmill that you can't take a break from? We overcommit ourselves and rush from one place to the next, rarely taking a breath, utterly exhausted and worn out.

The best way I know to combat this enemy is to develop a vision and set of core values for your life that you can filter your decision-making process through. Written on a three-by-five note card that I carry in my journal and look at nearly every day are three objectives I want to fulfill in my lifetime: I want to be known as a man who followed Christ, led his wife and family well, and was a faithful pastor to a local church. There is nothing I'd love more than to accomplish these three objectives. By looking at them every day, I am constantly reminded of what is *most* important. When the enemy of busyness comes knocking, this set of core values helps me determine what I allow onto my calendar and ultimately what I accept or reject.

Enemy #2—Complacency

Routine is important for raising children, but it's also important for the practice of spiritual disciplines. My personal routine does not vary that much. I have had the habit for years of waking up and spending time alone with the Lord. I wake up around the same time each morning. I typically eat the same thing at the same time at the same place from week to week. But there was a season of my life when my time alone with the Lord had grown stale. It became about checking something off a list instead of about sitting at the feet of Jesus. I found myself just going through the motions spiritually. I was just getting by in my relationship with the Lord, and I had grown lethargic and lackadaisical as it related to pursuing him. Tozer addressed this lack in my life, writing,

> The stiff and wooden quality about our religious lives is a result of our lack of holy desire. Complacency is a deadly foe of all spiritual growth. . . .

The shallowness of our inner experience, the hollowness of our worship, and that servile imitation of the world which marks our promotional methods all testify that we, in this day, know God only imperfectly, and the peace of God scarcely at all.[5]

Ouch! *Stiff. Wooden. Complacent. Shallow. Hollow.* These are the words that described what I was feeling in my heart, and it was driving me crazy. I was so frustrated in my walk with the Lord. My worship was not passionate. My service had no enthusiasm. My prayer life was not vibrant. I was sharing my faith out of obligation, not out of joy from within.

What happened to the excitement that I had when I first entered my personal relationship with Christ? When had I started to settle spiritually? This process of growing complacent didn't happen overnight. It crept up on me, and I didn't even notice it.

I liken it to what it was like when my buddies and I would go tubing in college. All you need to float down a river is an inner tube; that's it! You sit in the inner tube, and the river does the rest. The drift happens naturally. You flow with the current of the water.

The same is true with complacency when it comes to our spirituality. It's natural to drift away from the Lord.

And this is why complacency is so dangerous and such an enemy of intimacy. Because it's insidious in nature. It happens when we are not even aware of it.

Enemy #3—Comfort

The truth is, in seasons when I'm not going to the mountain to pray, it's because I'm unwilling to pay the price to know God in a deeper and more personal way. I become comfortable just getting by, just existing. And my desire for comfort and ease strangles any chance of experiencing intimacy with the Lord.

I soon learned that comfort and ease are the opposite of cross bearing. Remember the words of Jesus?

> Then Jesus told his disciples, "If anyone would come after me, let him deny himself and take up his cross and follow me. For whoever would save his life will lose it, but whoever loses his life for my sake will find it." (Matthew 16:24–25)

The call of Christ is not a call to comfort but a call to die. Being comfortable and climbing the mountain can't coexist. Comfort and cross bearing are not compatible. I constantly have to remind myself of this truth. I don't like leaving my comfort zone. Do you know why? Because it's comfortable! I don't like being stretched too far in my faith. It makes me uncomfortable.

After a long day at work, I would rather come home, pull into the garage, let the garage doors down, walk inside the house, and go watch television. That's comfortable. But God calls me to deny myself this life of ease and go meet my neighbors and love them in his name.

When I am at a coffee shop or restaurant, I would rather keep to myself. That's comfortable. But God calls me out of my comfort zone to speak to and serve others with the hope of having a gospel conversation with them.

We can't let a life of ease and comfort keep us from intimacy with God. If Abraham had been after a life of ease and comfort, there is no way he would have answered God's call to Mount Moriah. If Elijah had wanted a comfortable life, he would not have confronted Ahab and challenged the prophets of Baal on Mount Carmel.

Answering the call to intimacy is never easy. I pastored young singles and college students for nearly ten years. It always amazed me to meet with young men who were laser-focused on their careers. They would get to the office early and stay at the office late if that's what it took to get the job done. They were competitive in everything they did. From playing intramurals to setting up their fantasy football teams, their mind-set was focused and their determination strong. They were consumed with their physical appearance. They would work out, watch their diet, and come to church dressed in their Sunday best. After all, they never knew when they would come across "the one."

When it came to their spiritual growth, though, when it came to fostering their relationship with God, it was perplexing to see these same people think that intimacy with God just happens, as by osmosis or something. It doesn't just happen. It takes work.

For us to grow in intimacy with God, we must give our whole

hearts toward the effort. We can't afford to let a life of comfort and ease keep us from breaking away from the crowds and ascending the mountain to know God.

All Is Well

Jesus routinely went out to the mountains to pray. This time with his Father was vital for his life and work. If the Son of God had to have it, then it's a safe bet we do too. These intimate times with God are when the Father revives and restores us. It's when he whispers in our hearts and shows us the way. It's on these desolate mountains with God that he grants us wisdom and gives us direction.

Remember Riley's story? Debbie and I made a commitment after leaving the restaurant that evening that if it was in our power, we would never put ourselves in a situation like that again. Chaos ensued because we got Riley off her routine. And that chaos was as bad for Riley as it was for us. It put all of us in a no-win situation.

I've found that what's true for Riley is true for me. If I get out of my routine of getting to the mountain to pray and spend time alone with God, then chaos ensues. Nothing seems to go right for me and often for those around me. Things just seem to be a bit off. The bottom line is I'm like a child, and I need to stay on a routine spiritually. When I do, all is well.

What about you? Is all well in your life? If within you feel a bit chaotic, if there is no peace when you pillow your head, then maybe the first step is to start your journey toward the Mount Desolate. Identify what's in the way, and ask God to help you remove it from being a barrier. You'll discover that a little time spent routinely on this mountain can change your life and maybe even the life of those around you.

Mount Eremos

The God Who Is Father

A group from my church decided to visit India in 2005. We purposely went northeast, where Christianity was almost absent. We went to the state of Uttar Pradesh, visiting cities like Varanasi, Agra, and Allahabad.

The country was beautiful, and it was easy to fall in love with the people and their rich history. Their hospitality was remarkable, and we sensed the people were, for the most part, genuinely glad to see us touring their country. We visited some of the most holy sites in Hinduism and floated down the Ganges River, the holy river of the Hindus. We saw men and women along the river bank baptizing themselves, believing the act would wash away their sins. We witnessed people bathing, washing their clothes, and performing religious rituals of all kinds. We even saw the wrapped remains of a dead Hindu priest floating in the river.

It was sensory overload for me. The trip was spiritually and emotionally exhilarating while at the same time absolutely exhausting. There is no doubt it's the darkest place spiritually that I've ever been. Looking into the people's eyes, I could sense the hopelessness and desperation. I've seen poverty in the inner city of Dallas, but nothing could compare to what I witnessed on the streets of India. People living on the sides of the roads, sleeping on the ground with nothing but a cardboard box to cover them.

One of the most moving parts of the trip for me was meeting a young boy at an orphanage. He could not have been older than three years of age. His story was like a punch in the gut to me. He'd been found by the orphanage in a nearby dumpster. He was blind in his left eye because a hungry dog had found him before the orphanage did.

We met this boy and visited his orphanage about midway through our trip. We'd already toured some of the temples, seen the rampant idol worship and evil that was pervasive in the culture. Darkness surrounded us, and in all that darkness, this little boy had gone unnoticed.

How did this boy get to this point? What would cause a mom or dad or relative to place him in the dumpster and leave him to die? Where was God in this? Had he forgotten about the people of India? Had he forgotten about this little boy? And if he was forgotten, couldn't any of us find ourselves in the same predicament? I grew more than a little depressed at what I saw, and I didn't like where my mind went.

Forgotten by God?

People don't like to think that they've been forgotten, but this is exactly how the people of Israel felt in Jesus's day. From the time of Abraham, God had promised to be with them. He gave his word that he would make them into a great nation and that they would be his "treasured possession." It was first given as the Abrahamic promise of Genesis 12, often recalled by the Israelites:

> Now the LORD said to Abram, "Go from your country and your kindred and your father's house to the land that I will

show you. And I will make of you a great nation, and I will bless you and make your name great, so that you will be a blessing." (verses 1–2)

Not only had God promised that he would make them into a great nation, but he also promised that a deliverer would come, a Messiah to bring about this greatness they so desperately wanted. The Hebrew nation looked back to the words given to Moses and put their hope in them:

I will raise up for them a prophet like you from among their brothers. And I will put my words in his mouth, and he shall speak to them all that I command him. (Deuteronomy 18:18)

But there they were, subjects of Roman rule, and no prophet like Moses had come. No king had ascended to David's throne. And for years, the people of Israel waited.

To make matters worse, there were no current prophets, not really. In the Old Testament, the Jewish people had a revolving door of prophets forecasting future events. They were at least hearing from God through men like Isaiah and Jeremiah. By the time of the New Testament, though, God had been silent for over four hundred years.

There can be no doubt; the people were disillusioned and cynical about the promises of God. Sure, they had heard the stories of the faithfulness of God in the past, but that was ancient history to them. God must have moved on. Their question was a fair one: "God, have you forgotten us?"

That's when Jesus showed up. And unlike the scribes and Pharisees, Jesus seemed to care about the hearts of the people. He looked them in the eyes and touched them when they were sick. He healed diseases and went about doing good. He preached a message that God and his kingdom had finally come. People flocked to Jesus. And though the people certainly wanted to see this miracle-working prophet, they also wanted to hear him teach.

And teach Jesus did. His first and longest teaching discourse recorded in Scripture is his Sermon on the Mount. Matthew recorded it like this:

> Seeing the crowds, he went up on the mountain, and when he sat down, his disciples came to him.
>
> And he opened his mouth and taught them. (Matthew 5:1–2)

Prayer *Is* Relationship

On a mountainside in Galilee, Jesus taught his first sermon, a sermon about the coming kingdom of God. It was there on the mountain that he introduced the disciples and surrounding crowd to a new perspective of God, a groundbreaking revelation. He used prayer as an illustration to deliver these truths. Read what

Jesus spoke to the crowd that day:

Pray then like this:

"Our Father in heaven,
hallowed be your name.
Your kingdom come,
your will be done,
    on earth as it is in heaven.
Give us this day our daily bread,
and forgive us our debts,
    as we also have forgiven our debtors.
And lead us not into temptation,
    but deliver us from evil." (Matthew 6:9–13)

Those listening to Jesus teach were, of course, quite familiar with prayer. Prayer was foundational in the Jewish culture. The people practiced prayer in the local synagogue and in their homes. It was a common custom among the faithful. But Jesus wanted them to understand the true nature of prayer. He wanted to make sure that his followers avoided two extremes when it came to praying. First, he did not want them to make prayer a public spectacle, like those he labeled as hypocrites. Second, he wanted to make sure that their prayers were not mechanical, that they were something more than the monotonous repetitions of the Gentiles.

Jesus emphasized to them that prayer was not to be a mindless ritual or an exercise of piety on a public platform but rather the means to a relationship with him. Jesus wanted the crowd to know that God wasn't distant. He was near, he was concerned about their needs, and he wanted to provide for those he considered his children.

What better way to teach them about prayer than by way of a prayer, a model of sorts, one they could use as a guide? Jesus said, "Pray then like this." And this is how the model prayer begins: *Our Father in heaven.*

Father. In Aramaic it's the word *Abba,* which means "daddy." Seventeen times in this sermon, Jesus used this word to describe God. It's used only nine times in all the Old Testament. Jesus was making a strong point regarding the relationship God has with those in his family.

There's not a better word in the English language to me than *daddy.* I'm having the hardest time completing this chapter because my five-year-olds keep coming in screaming, "Daddy, Daddy!" Their to-do list for me includes playing with them, coloring with them, watching TV with them, reading to them. They just want time with their dad. To think that I can approach and speak to God as my little girls approach and speak to me is overwhelming. But it's true. He is our "Abba" daddy, and just as I love to hear the voice of my girls, God loves hearing the voice of his children, your voice and mine.

God is awesome and infinite. He is immortal and authoritative. But he is also our Father, tender and caring, welcoming and accessible.

But God isn't just any kind of father. His is a specific reality. He's our holy Father: *hallowed be your name.* We don't use the word *hallow* much these days. It's a word that means "to reverence as holy." It is to render something or someone as sacred. When we hallow the name of God, we are recognizing that he is not ordinary. He is separate and distinct, seemingly unapproachable in his holiness. He's not unapproachable, though, as we have seen. This God we hallow continually invites us into his presence and longs to spend time with us. Simply amazing!

His name—holy Father—encompasses his character; it's the sum total of who he is. Jesus wanted to share a truth with the crowd on the mountain that day: God is a loving Father, but he is also completely set apart, completely holy, and to be honored, praised, and held in the highest regard.

Jesus could have stopped there, and that would have been more than enough to shake the minds and hearts of the people. But he didn't stop. From there the prayer transitions to its first request: *Your kingdom come.*

The coming kingdom of God is what the ministry of Jesus was all about. Following his baptism, he preached, "Repent, for the kingdom of heaven is at hand" (Matthew 4:17). The kingdom can be defined as the rule and reign of God, and it has both a present and a future connotation to it.

There have always been two competing kingdoms in the world: the kingdom of darkness and the kingdom of light. In making this request part of the model prayer, Jesus taught the people to pray for their Father's kingdom to rule and reign, to prevail in their lives as individuals and in all creation.

In prayer we ask for God's will to be done: *Your will be done, on earth as it is in heaven.*

Jesus wanted the people to know that God's will was not hidden from them. This was one of the primary reasons Jesus came to the earth. He was the revelation of God's will on earth. He modeled what it meant to submit to God's will. Jesus knew that a real relationship with God began with a heart surrendered to the will of the Father, and as we walk with him in relationship, he reveals more and more of his will to us.

The request for provision follows: *Give us this day our daily bread.*

The point of this request is to express a dependence on God to meet and supply daily needs. Jesus knew that most of those sitting on the mountainside that day were poor. They had little to nothing. They probably didn't even know where their next meal was coming from. Jesus did. He knew that God, the loving, holy Father, wanted to meet their needs, even the most basic of needs, like food and clothing.

Jesus also knew that to live full and satisfying lives, his disciples would need right relationships with God and with others, so he taught them to pray and ask God for forgiveness and the ability to forgive others: *And forgive us our debts, as we also have forgiven our debtors.*

Sin and the guilt of sin weighed people down. God could

meet the outward and circumstantial needs of their lives, but what they needed most was forgiveness. They knew this but always thought forgiveness of sin came when they made the right sacrifices. Jesus brought with him a revolutionary perspective. He came teaching that forgiveness is granted when God's followers confess their sins to him in humility and then repent, willfully choosing to forgive others for offenses committed against them.

Then from forgiveness to protection: *And lead us not into temptation, but deliver us from evil.*

On the mountain, Jesus showed us the spiritual battle that was hidden from the physical eyes of those who followed him. He made us aware of the insidious Enemy of our souls. He taught that the people could appeal to God, their loving Abba, and he would protect them from the evil and oppression that surrounded them, just as a good earthly father would protect his children.

Jesus brought a change of perspective on that mountain. He taught the people that they had access to God and could connect to him as an earthly child would connect to his earthly father. It would have boggled their minds to think that God wanted a relationship with them, that he might desire a relationship with them through the act of prayer. Prayer wasn't impersonal and perfunctory. Instead it was a deeply personal privilege, an opportunity to really know God.

Surely some of those listening to Jesus's teaching that day thought it sounded too good to be true. For some of us it may still sound that way today.

Too Good to Be True

Jesus began his ministry with this mountainside sermon, and he left the people with this impression: *God wants a familial relationship with us.* He is not like other gods, those fickle taskmasters ready to judge and punish. He is a loving Father ready to receive his children with open arms. That was the point of Jesus's Sermon on the Mount—to fundamentally change the people's notion of God.

But like always, God's desire was also to change the people's notion of themselves. He wanted them to see that they were dearly loved children. He wanted to show them that by childlike faith, they might enter a relationship with him that came with all the rights and privileges of blood. And the rest of the Scriptures bear this truth out. John recorded in his gospel, "As many as received Him, to them He gave the right to become children of God, even to those who believe in His name" (1:12, NASB).

Paul wrote to the Galatians, "You are all sons of God through faith in Christ Jesus" (3:26, NASB).

It is by faith in Jesus and belief in his name that we enter a relationship with God. This is how he becomes a personal Father to us and how we become part of his family. And what's most amazing? God's invitation into a relationship with him is for everyone. It's totally inclusive. It's for the up-and-up and the down-and-out. It's for the outcast in this world, but it's also for the elite. It's for all people willing to humble themselves and come, regardless of age, gender, ethnicity, or social status. Jesus's mountainside sermon in Galilee proved once and for all that God is a God for the people, and he welcomes a relationship with everyone.

As if it weren't enough to be part of his family, Jesus also showed us that we are royal children, whom God has invited to participate in his kingdom. Consider the words of Paul: "He has delivered us from the domain of darkness and transferred us to the kingdom of his beloved Son, in whom we have redemption, the forgiveness of sins" (Colossians 1:13–14).

We become kingdom citizens and get to play a part in bringing the rule and reign of Christ to the world. Wherever we go and whatever we do, we are his representatives. We are his emissaries, bringing light to darkness. Jesus said we are to make his kingdom a priority in our lives, that we are to help expand his kingdom by sharing what it's about with others.

Every son and daughter of God has roles and responsibilities within the kingdom of God to bring about the King's will and desires. In teaching the disciples this prayer, Jesus was giving them an action plan for their lives. In teaching them to pray for his kingdom to come, he was giving them purpose and meaning, and offering an invitation to participate in his eternal, global enterprise.

Through the Sermon on the Mount, Jesus showed us that we are royal children and that *God takes care of those of us in his family.* In fact, half of this prayer is requests for provision, protection, and care. And later in this same sermon, Jesus made it even more clear:

Ask, and it will be given to you; seek, and you will find; knock, and it will be opened to you. For everyone who asks receives, and the one who seeks finds, and to the one who knocks it will be opened. Or which one of you, if his son asks him for bread, will give him a stone? Or if he asks for a fish, will give him a serpent? If you then, who are evil, know how to give good gifts to your children, how much more will your Father who is in heaven give good things to those who ask him! (Matthew 7:7–11)

God has always promised to take care of his children and meet the needs of those who follow him. He encourages us to bring our requests to him and to seek him in prayer. Please hear me. Underline this statement. Ponder this truth: God has not forgotten us.

Can a woman forget her nursing child,
    that she should have no compassion on
        the son of her womb?
Even these may forget,
    yet I will not forget you. (Isaiah 49:15)

It might be even better here if you personalize this. God has not forgotten you. And he never will. No matter what you are facing or what you may be up against, you are a royal child of the King and his eye is on you.

Adopted

I keep a photo of that little boy I met in India back in 2005 on the desk in my office. It turned out that his story had a pretty happy ending. Abandoned and left for dead, this little boy had a future that didn't look too promising. Most people would have written him off and considered him to be another statistic, just another abandoned child who was forgotten and didn't make it.

But the directors of that Christian orphanage found him and took him in. They showered him with love and got him the medical attention he needed. In the picture on my desk, he is fully clothed, looking into my camera. He is wearing a very stoic look, having already faced more of an uphill battle in his three years of life than I have in nearly forty. What makes the picture special to me, though, is not really the boy but the adopted dad holding him. It's the smile on the father's face that gets me. You can see the happiness in the father's bright eyes, the father's huge smile; he is overjoyed and proud to be holding his son.

I was foolish to ever think that God had forgotten this boy. And this picture that I often look at reminds me that God will never forget me. This is the essence of the revelation on Mount Eremos. God is our loving Father. We are his beloved children. And God will never forget us.

Mount Hermon

The God Who Is Jesus

As I write this chapter, I am sitting in Thailand about to speak to over two hundred missionaries who are currently serving Christ overseas. They live and work in some of the most remote and hard-to-reach places on the planet, many of which are behind borders closed to the gospel. Some have been turned away from countries they were working in and been blacklisted from ever returning. Their work is dangerous, and they are gathered at a retreat center for rest and to enjoy some extended time as families.

I have been deeply moved hearing some of their stories. Jason graduated from a small university and was serving in India. For years he was making progress in his work, leading people to Jesus, discipling new believers, and training indigenous pastors. When returning to India after a brief furlough in the States, he was met at customs and his visa was revoked. He was not allowed to gather his things. He was not allowed to clean out his house, say goodbye to his associates, or continue the work he'd invested in for years. He and his family were forced to go to another country and essentially start their ministry over from scratch.

When he was telling me this story, he was in good spirits and nearly laughing about it, treating it as if this sort of stuff happens all the time. Stories like his are common among these missionaries, and I was inspired and amazed by the faith of these men and women and their families. But I've been away from my family for nearly ten days, and I miss them tremendously. I'm ready to see my girls again. I miss them even more when I scroll through the photos on my phone and see their faces. I've been able to Face-Time with them when the Wi-Fi connection is good, and these interactions do wonders for my spirit.

It's pretty amazing to think about, isn't it? Though a distance of nearly nine thousand miles separates us and though we are twenty hours apart, I am still able to see them and communicate with them. It's one thing to look at my photos and think about my wife and the girls, but to see their faces on-screen and hear their voices? It makes me long for them even more.

In the seeing, our desire for connection grows stronger. Maybe this is why Jesus led Peter, James, and John to Mount Hermon, the place of the Transfiguration. He wanted them to see who he really was and to long even more for that stronger connection.

Jesus's True Identity

Identity. It is one of the buzzwords in our current culture. It was in Jesus's time too. There was a lot of debate about his identity. No one could seem to figure out who he was. He showed up on the scene casting out demons, healing diseases, spending time with outcasts, and challenging the religious authorities of the day. If that was not enough, he actually claimed to be the Son of God. And while he made this claim, only his small band of disciples really believed him, and at times even they had their doubts.

Who was Jesus? His own family thought he was crazy. Early in his ministry, as his popularity spread, people began to follow him everywhere. He performed miracles and healed a number of people from diseases. But his family didn't know what to do about his notoriety. When he arrived in his hometown, so many people followed him that his family went to get him, telling people, "He is out of his mind" (Mark 3:21).

Who was Jesus? The religious leaders labeled him a heretic. As far as we know, only one, Nicodemus, came to him seeking answers to his questions, and even then it was under the cover of night. Nicodemus wanted to know the true identity of Jesus. Who was he? Where did he come from?

Even King Herod wondered about Jesus. When he first heard about the miracles and ministry of Jesus, it caused him to be confused. Herod was perplexed and wondered if Jesus was Elijah or John the Baptist reincarnated.

Who was Jesus? That was the question of the day, and it's the same question Jesus posed to his disciples before the mountain experience we call the Transfiguration. Luke recorded that conversation this way:

Now it happened that as he was praying alone, the disciples were with him. And he asked them, "Who do the crowds say that I am?" And they answered, "John the Baptist. But others say, Elijah, and others, that one of the prophets of old has risen." Then he said to them, "But who do you say that I am?" And Peter answered, "The Christ of God." (Luke 9:18–20)

Rumor and speculation were everywhere, but here Peter confirmed that Jesus is the Messiah. And immediately upon this confession of faith, Jesus affirmed Peter's confession.

> Jesus answered him, "Blessed are you, Simon Bar-Jonah!
> For flesh and blood has not revealed this to you, but my
> Father who is in heaven." (Matthew 16:17)

That should have settled it, right? His identity clearly heard in words. Jesus affirms the confession. But then Jesus went one step further. Rather than just sharing with him his identity, he was getting read to show them his identity. Jesus took his inner circle of friends—Peter, James, and John—up the mountain so that he might reveal himself in HD. They were about to get a glimpse of Jesus that no one living at that time had ever seen before. And what they saw and experienced on that mountain would change them forever.

> Now about eight days after these sayings he took with him
> Peter and John and James and went up on the mountain to
> pray. And as he was praying, the appearance of his face was
> altered, and his clothing became dazzling white. And
> behold, two men were talking with him, Moses and Elijah,
> who appeared in glory and spoke of his departure, which
> he was about to accomplish at Jerusalem. Now Peter and
> those who were with him were heavy with sleep, but when

they became fully awake they saw his glory and the two men who stood with him. And as the men were parting from him, Peter said to Jesus, "Master, it is good that we are here. Let us make three tents, one for you and one for Moses and one for Elijah"—not knowing what he said. As he was saying these things, a cloud came and overshadowed them, and they were afraid as they entered the cloud. And a voice came out of the cloud, saying, "This is my Son, my Chosen One; listen to him!" And when the voice had spoken, Jesus was found alone. And they kept silent and told no one in those days anything of what they had seen. (Luke 9:28–36)

It's important to remember that up to this point in Scripture, outside of the authoritative teaching and the miracles that Jesus performed, there had been nothing to indicate that Jesus was any different from anyone else living at the time. He certainly didn't appear different. In fact, the prophet Isaiah described Jesus as one having "no form or majesty that we should look at him, and no beauty that we should desire him" (53:2). Unlike the old artists' renderings of him, Jesus did not walk around with a halo and bright light exuding from his head. There was no holy glow about him!

Outside of his miracles, which many probably wrote off as coincidences or attributed to the devil, nothing would have caused anyone to look up and take notice of Jesus. He seemed just like everyone else.

When Jesus was hungry, he ate.

When Jesus was tired, he slept.

When Jesus needed strength, he prayed.

When Jesus received the news that his friend John the Baptist was murdered, he grieved.

In other words, the deity of Jesus was completely veiled when he walked the earth. As John wrote, "The Word became *flesh* and dwelt among us" (John 1:14, emphasis added).

What's more, Jesus didn't come in some great show of power. Instead, consider the words of Paul, who taught that Jesus "emptied" himself, putting it like this in the book of Philippians: "who, though he [Jesus] was in the form of God, did not count equality with God a thing to be grasped, but emptied himself, by taking the form of a servant, being born in the likeness of men" (2:6–7). The *NIV Study Bible* annotation that goes with verse 7 describes Jesus becoming utterly human as him "laying aside his glory . . . and submitting to the humiliation of becoming man."[6]

The Scriptures teach that Jesus walked the earth as God incognito. He willingly surrendered the glory he held in eternity as the Son of God and entered space and time to identify with man. But as if to remove any doubt—the doubt of either the disciples or you and me all these years later—Jesus ascended the Mount of Transfiguration to show his true identity. Peter, James, and John saw his glory in full, and through their experience, we get a glimpse of his glory as well.

On the mountain, the disciples witnessed the holiest shift in perspective about Jesus. They saw him in his eternal glory, the glory he surrendered to come to earth. They saw Moses and Elijah, two figures representing all law and the prophets, confirming that he was the perfect fulfillment of God's Word. They heard and saw Jesus for who he was and is and forever will be.

This revelation is so important that Luke, Matthew, and Mark all share it with differing details.

> As he was praying, the appearance of his face was altered,
> and his clothing became dazzling white. (Luke 9:29)

> He was transfigured before them, and his face shone like
> the sun. (Matthew 17:2)

> He was transfigured before them, and his clothes became
> radiant, intensely white, as no one on earth could bleach
> them. (Mark 9:2–3)

In these texts, Jesus's spiritual reality broke into the world of men for the first time! This is the Transfiguration.

Transfiguration—what does it mean? The word means "to be changed." The Greek word is the source of the English word *metamorphosis*. If you're a science buff, think caterpillar to butterfly. If you're the literary type, think Gregor from Franz Kafka's novella *The Metamorphosis*. If you were a kid in the 1980s (like me), think Incredible Hulk! But whatever your reference point, know this: the Transfiguration indicates a radical transformation. Jesus changed right before the eyes of those three disciples. His deity was completely unveiled.

Reflection or Radiation?

Remember how we defined the glory of God from the experience Moses had on Mount Sinai after the Israelites left Egypt? God's glory is the epitome of who he is. The word means "weight or heaviness." Moses had been in the presence of God for forty days and then descended with the tablets we know as the Ten Commandments.

> When Moses came down from Mount Sinai, with the two
> tablets of the testimony in his hand as he came down from
> the mountain, Moses did not know that the skin of his
> face shone because he had been talking with God.
> (Exodus 34:29)

In this scriptural account, Moses reflected the glory of God. But that's not how it was in the Transfiguration. On that mountain, Jesus radiated the glory of God. This is a significant difference. It's the difference between the sun, which radiates light, and the moon, which only reflects the sun's light. One is the source; the other gives witness to the source.

What a transformative moment the Transfiguration was.

God the Father in a moment in time revealed the glory of Jesus to three disciples and spoke directly to them concerning his nature. Jesus was not just a great servant or a chosen prophet; he was God's Son. Peter, James, and John were given a new perspective, one that answers the question, Who is Jesus?

But as we've seen with each mountaintop revelation, there is also new insight about us, the people of God. The disciples gained new insights into themselves, into their position before the glorified Christ. Mark's account mentions that Peter, James, and John were terrified and that they didn't know what to do or say. They were overwhelmed, first with fear, but their fear soon gave way to wonder. Elijah, Moses, and Jesus together—no one had seen this before. And as they watched, they realized that there was nothing to fear in God's presence. Yes, "perfect love casts out fear" (1 John 4:18). In this realization, their hearts were thrilled with wonder and awe. They did not want what they were witnessing to end.

Peter said what they all must have been thinking: "Let's build some tents for us! Let's stay here!" But the moment would not last. Luke said that after God spoke, Elijah and Moses disappeared and "Jesus was found alone" (9:36). Matthew's account puts it this way: "When they lifted up their eyes, they saw no one but Jesus only" (17:8). Mark wrote, "Suddenly, looking around, they no longer saw anyone with them but Jesus only" (9:8).

And then there was one. Jesus only. This is the point of what the three disciples experienced on Mount Hermon. God reveals the glory of his Son and shows that there is none greater than him.

Not the great lawgiver, Moses, or the great prophet Elijah. Jesus has no rival. In the words of one commentator, "The primary purpose of Moses and Elijah was to salute their divine Successor, and then to leave Him alone in His unchallenged supremacy, the sole object of His disciples' veneration."[7]

I love that phrase: *unchallenged supremacy.* This is the perspective we receive from the Mount of Transfiguration. It is Jesus alone who commands our worship and devotion. And knowing this truth and experiencing it personally are the heart of veneration, of intimacy.

Who Do *You* Say Jesus Is?

What about you? What's keeping you from seeing Jesus clearly? Are you relying on the thoughts and opinions of others to show you who Jesus is? Are you so caught up in Bible studies and the sermons of your favorite preachers that you tend to lean more on what they have to say about Jesus rather than listening to and seeing him for yourself? Spiritually, this is blurry vision at best. You can learn from others, no doubt, but the question is ultimately posed to you: Who do *you* say Jesus is?

This is why we must ascend the mountain. We must see Jesus for ourselves. When we see him clearly, yes, our perspective of God is changed, and on the mountain, our perspective of ourselves will also be changed. We find that God invites us into the fullness of his presence, and we can stand in the wonder of his glory without being afraid.

I love the Transfiguration because it's a foretaste of heaven. It's like getting an appetizer before the meal. The appetizer is not meant to fill you up; it's just meant to satisfy you until the meal arrives. In the Transfiguration, we get a glimpse of what heaven is going to be like. We will be with Jesus and see him as he is in his unveiled glory.

Coming Home

Twenty-one hours. That's how long the flight was from Bangkok, Thailand, to Dallas, Texas. I thought it would never end. There are only so many movies you can watch and naps you can take. Finally, after landing, I went through the process of gathering my bags and walking off the plane. After making it through customs, I hurried out the exit of the terminal. It more than made my day seeing all my girls running up to hug me and welcome me home.

Sure, I had their pictures with me while I was in Thailand. I even spoke with them via FaceTime on a few occasions while overseas. But that didn't compare to being with them. It didn't compare to being able to put my arms around them, being able to sit down and read a book or play with them. This was something altogether different. I was actually with them, in their presence.

This difference is what Jesus invites us into. It's the reality of the Mount Hermon experience. He wants us to be in his presence, with him. He wants to show us his glory. He longs to reveal to us exactly who he is, and for us to stand unafraid in wonder and worship before him.

The great news is that Jesus can hardly wait for you to know him in this way. My desire to see my wife and daughters after my long trip was off the charts. But Jesus's desire for you to come home to his goodness and grace? To be in his presence? It is infinitely greater. All you have to do is start climbing.

Mount Olivet

The God Who Is Near

B o, Craig, and I were best friends. In elementary school, we called ourselves "the Three Amigos." Bo's mom even had our self-imposed moniker along with a picture of the three of us printed on matching T-shirts. A little embarrassing looking back on it, but we wore them with pride back in the day. The three of us did everything together. We played on the same ball teams, spent the night at one another's houses, and got beaten up by one another's older brothers. We were inseparable.

Bo's dad served in the air force. I'll never forget when Bo told me his family was being transferred. My friend Bo would be moving. I couldn't believe it. The Three Amigos were breaking up, but we knew we would see one another again. And we did. Every summer through our elementary and junior high years, our parents made a special effort to get us together to hang out. As we got into high school, though, our time was consumed with sports and studies, and it became harder and harder to schedule time together. By college, we rarely saw one another. We were growing up and had our own lives.

There were no cell phones back then, no Twitter or Facebook, so staying in touch was a challenge, but we did manage to reconnect from time to time. I was grateful because it never took long to pick up where we'd left off. I thought it would always be this way, that even from distances we'd always be in one another's lives. That is, until I received a phone call.

Heading into my junior year of college, I was taking some

summer courses and working a part-time job at a sporting goods store near the campus. I came home from my morning classes one day, and the phone rang as I walked in the door. On the other end of the line, I could hear Mrs. Lisa, Bo's mom, sobbing.

"My Bo, my Bo," she repeated over and over again.

I stood there in the small kitchen of my apartment bracing myself, and the waiting felt like an eternity. Whatever the news, I knew it wasn't good. It was one of those moments when my heart seemed to stop. Time slowed down. I could feel my labored breathing. I'll never forget her words, the hurt I heard in her voice as she spoke, and my shock.

In the days following that conversation, I'd learn the details of Bo's death. He was an athlete and avid water-skier. Growing up, we'd often get to the nearest lake to ski. Bo could slalom better than any of us, and he loved to do what we called "fishtailing." From outside the wake, he'd lean out over his ski and make a sharp turn, which would spray water on unsuspecting people idling on a boat or deck nearby. Everyone he sprayed seemed to appreciate the humor of getting soaking wet, especially during those hot and humid summer days in Louisiana.

The day before Mrs. Lisa called, Bo was skiing and went to fishtail a boat nearby. It was something he'd done probably a hundred times before. This time, though, he'd misjudged how close he was to the other boat, and he broadsided it, knocking himself unconscious. He was rushed to medical care, but the impact caused his lungs to collapse. Bo never woke up. He died the next day, the same day I spoke to his mom. Tragedy had come to Bo's family, and that included me.

Mountaintop or Valley?

More often than not, when we think about mountaintop moments or experiences, we think positive thoughts. We don't think about the tough times, the trials we go through. We consider those the valleys, the low times in life. Those dark and lonely times, though, can bring us to a fuller understanding of God, a richer experience of him. They can be their own sort of midnight mountaintop experience.

In a book about the mountains in Scripture, you probably wouldn't think a garden would make an appearance, especially the Garden of Gethsemane. But here it is. Jesus had just finished celebrating Passover and sharing the Lord's Supper with his disciples. After "they had sung a hymn" (Matthew 26:30), Jesus led them across the Kidron Valley. They made their way to a mountain called Olivet or, as we've come to call it, the Mount of Olives.

He came out and went, as was his custom, to the Mount of Olives, and the disciples followed him. And when he came to the place, he said to them, "Pray that you may not enter into temptation." And he withdrew from them about a stone's throw, and knelt down and prayed, saying, "Father, if you are willing, remove this cup from me. Nevertheless,

not my will, but yours, be done." And there appeared to
him an angel from heaven, strengthening him. And being
in agony he prayed more earnestly; and his sweat became
like great drops of blood falling down to the ground.
(Luke 22:39–44)

I've always been fascinated with this picture of Jesus in the
Garden of Gethsemane. He knew he was about to be betrayed,
arrested by the authorities, and put to death in the impending
hours. And yet he still chose to go to the place where his journey
to the cross would begin. He chose Gethsemane, a garden on a
mountain, as the starting place for the Passion narrative.

Compared with the sights and sounds of the city of Jerusalem, Gethsemane was quiet and serene, especially during that
time of the evening. The garden had always been a place of refuge
for Jesus. It was "his custom" to go there and pray. This prayer
time was different, though. And the disciples who followed him to
the garden on the mountain may not have fully realized it, but I
want to believe they knew something was different.

Mark's gospel notes that Jesus began to be "greatly distressed
and troubled," saying to the disciples he'd invited up the mountain, "My soul is very sorrowful, even to death" (14:33–34). Why?

In the hours before his arrest and crucifixion, he was surely
feeling the burden of his coming death. He was aware that the
judgment of sin would be on his shoulders and that a baptism in
the wrath of God awaited him. He sensed a coming chasm in the
eternal fellowship he had shared with God the Father from before

the beginning of time. It was an overwhelming assignment, and he felt the weight, crushing him as if in an olive press. He was to be poured out like oil.

This is the first time we see Jesus this emotionally distraught, this anxious, and he'd encountered some bizarre situations before. He faced a raging storm on the Sea of Galilee and was composed the entire time. In fact, he slept through most of the whole thing. He was confronted with demoniacs on occasion. He battled temptation against the actual devil in the wilderness. He also had more than one collision with the religious leaders of the day who wanted to run him out of town, if not silence him for good.

In every instance, Jesus never appeared to be stressed out or on edge. He was in complete control. But here, in the garden, Jesus was more than a little concerned. He was deeply troubled, so much so that he fell to the ground, sweating drops of blood. He prayed to his Father to intervene, to do something.

What a moving description of Jesus. When I read this passage, it conjures up images of being in a dark room that is unfamiliar and trying to feel one's way around. The uncertainty one feels in that moment, the fear. The darkness was nearly unbearable. It was so intense he asked God for a way out, praying, "Father, if you are willing, remove this cup from me."

"This cup" is language and terminology that would have been very familiar to a Jewish audience. A person's "cup" in the Old Testament was considered to be whatever God determined to give that person; it represented the person's portion in life.

In Psalm 23:5, the psalmist spoke of his cup that "overflows," implying that the psalmist had been given more than enough blessing. More often than not, the "cup" was used to describe suffering and heartache. It refers to the wrath and judgment of God. Consider its use throughout the Old Testament:

> Let him [the LORD] rain coals on the wicked;
>> fire and sulfur and a scorching wind shall be the
>>> portion of their cup. (Psalm 11:6)

> Wake yourself, wake yourself,
>> stand up, O Jerusalem,
> you who have drunk from the hand of the LORD
>> the cup of his wrath,
> who have drunk to the dregs
>> the bowl, the cup of staggering. (Isaiah 51:17)

> The LORD, the God of Israel, said to me: "Take from my hand this cup of the wine of wrath, and make all the nations to whom I send you drink it. They shall drink and stagger and be crazed because of the sword that I am sending among them." (Jeremiah 25:15–16)

This cup Jesus didn't want to drink was the cup of God's wrath. Taking of this cup was the result of bearing the sins of the world. He was asking whether there was any way to secure mankind's salvation other than drinking the bitter brew of sin and judgment of God.

Jesus was not simply facing his physical death in that moment. He was readying himself to appease the wrath of God.

Easy Christianity

This picture of Jesus suffering in the Garden of Gethsemane shatters the idea that those who love God and walk with him will never endure heartache. In Scripture, Christian suffering is not the exception but the norm. Neither Jesus nor Paul pulled any punches about this. They told us this would be the case:

> In the world you will have tribulation. But take heart; I
> have overcome the world. (John 16:33)

> Indeed, all who desire to live a godly life in Christ Jesus
> will be persecuted. (2 Timothy 3:12)

Jesus never promised his followers easy and comfortable lives. He certainly didn't experience one himself. According to Open Doors, a ministry that seeks to serve persecuted Christians around the world, 255 Christians are killed every month for their faith.[8] Just because we don't see much visible suffering here in the West does not mean it is not happening around the world.

The Christian life is meant to be hard. The way of Jesus is the way of the Cross. Joining in "the fellowship of His sufferings" (Philippians 3:10, NASB) means that we will all have to spend some time on Mount Olivet in the Garden of Gethsemane.

We all suffer. And understanding this truth will help us as we inevitably walk through tough times. In times of suffering, our default question is usually some version of "Why? Why is God allowing me to suffer?" That's a fair question, and as we will see in a moment, it's okay to ask. I've asked that before and no doubt will again. But I have found that a better question to ask is "Could this be a midnight mountaintop moment, a season in which God wants to teach me something about himself, about me?"

A Bad Trade

As a pastor, I've walked alongside so many people experiencing the "dark night of the soul." These dark nights may spring from a divorce or an unwelcome diagnosis from a doctor. I've held hands with families who have lost a loved one to suicide and counseled elderly wives as their husbands are declining from Alzheimer's.

So often in these dark nights, the sufferer wants a word of encouragement or for me to say something that might bring them a little bit of peace. But I have found that it is often best to say nothing at all in these situations. Typically what they need more than anything is the "ministry of presence." They need someone who will simply be there with them, a listening ear, a shoulder to cry on. Over time, once the grief has set in and the original shock of what they are experiencing has abated a bit, I share with them a statement of truth that I heard from my pastor years ago:

Don't trade what you know for what you don't know.

Isn't this our tendency? When times of heartache and trouble come our way, don't we begin to trade certainties that we have never doubted for the uncertainties and unknowns that may or may not even exist?

You lose your job and your mind immediately races to *I'll never get hired again.* But that's an uncertainty. Don't trade the fact God is your provider for uncertainties that may or may not be the case.

Your relationship fractures and you assume *I'll never meet anyone else who could make me happy again.* But again, that's an uncertainty. Don't trade the fact that God knows and wants what is best for you for uncertainties that may or may not reflect reality.

Someone deeply offends you and you're convinced *I'll never be able to forgive him, and our relationship will never be what it once was.* That's an uncertainty. Don't trade the fact that God empowers you to forgive and over time can bring healing to any relationship for uncertainties that may or may not be true.

I'll say it again: *Don't trade what you know for what you don't know.*

Certainties on the Dark Mountain

In times of suffering, I refer to a list that comes directly from the life of Christ in the Garden of Gethsemane. This helps me climb my own mountain of suffering; it enables me to accept my struggle, to not try to trade it for what I don't know. This list is a constant reminder of certainties in the midst of suffering, and when I meditate on it in my own dark nights, I so often find the peace and presence of God.

Certainty #1—Suffering is universal and unavoidable

Suffering comes in all shapes and sizes. It doesn't matter where you are from—Jesus was from eternity, after all—what ethnicity you may be, how much you have or don't have. We live in a fallen world; we all suffer. No one is immune to it. But like Jesus, we can use it as an opportunity to meet with God on the mountain.

Certainty #2—Suffering is not a judgment for sin

This is perhaps the biggest lie we believe when we go through times of suffering. When we experience difficulty in life or go through a trial of some kind, it is very easy to think that God is judging us for our sin.

As believers, this could not be further from the truth. We may suffer due to the consequences of sinful decisions we make. If we choose to rebel against God or make a decision that is contrary to his Word and outside his will, we will reap what we sow. And sometimes the consequences of reaping what we sow are severe. God disciplines those he loves and chastises those whom he considers sons and daughters. But God does *not* send suffering as judgment for our sin. Jesus took our judgment with him to the cross.

Consider for a moment the teaching of Jesus in John's gospel about the man they came across who was born blind. The disciples thought his blindness must have been because of his sin or his parents' sin, and they questioned Jesus about it. The Lord's answer reveals that it was not because of sin that this man was born blind "but that the works of God might be displayed in him" (9:3).

God will use suffering as a tool to refine our faith and ultimately to bring him glory, but he does not send suffering as a tool to judge us for our sins. Doesn't Jesus's mountaintop experience with God in the garden show us as much?

Certainty #3—Suffering is temporary

Though it doesn't make it easier in the moment, it's good to remember that all suffering is temporary. Scripture says that we will suffer "a little while" (1 Peter 5:10), that we suffer only "light momentary affliction" (2 Corinthians 4:17), and that our sufferings are only for the "present time" (Romans 8:18).

At times we may think we'll never see light again. While we're in the middle of the dark night, though we may feel completely lost and utterly hopeless, we trust that Christ can resurrect anything. Just as Jesus was on the cross for six hours and in the grave for three days, there is a set limit to our suffering. It is temporary.

Certainty #4—God loves me and has not forgotten me

It's so easy to forget this truth when we are enduring hardship or are confronted with a tragedy of some kind. I offer you this certainty from God's Word. I used personal pronouns so that you could own its truth. God loves you and he has not forgotten you.

Who shall separate us from the love of Christ? Shall
tribulation, or distress, or persecution, or famine, or
nakedness, or danger, or sword? . . . No, in all these things
we are more than conquerors through him who loved us.
For I am sure that neither death nor life, nor angels nor
rulers, nor things present nor things to come, nor powers,
nor height nor depth, nor anything else in all creation, will
be able to separate us from the love of God in Christ Jesus
our Lord. (Romans 8:35, 37–39)

God promises that he "will never leave you nor forsake you"
and that he is "near to the brokenhearted and saves the crushed in
spirit." When we feel most alone and our hearts are the heaviest,
God is right there with us. Again, this is a matter of extreme trust.
Maybe this is why Jesus responded, "Father, . . . not my will, but
yours, be done." Even in the darkness of the mountain garden,
Jesus trusted that God was with him and entrusted his life to his
Father. He knew that God loved him and had not forgotten him.

Certainty #5—God empathizes with me in my suffering
Perhaps we don't often consider that God the Father suffered in
the garden as well. This was not a one-sided affair. The Father and
the Son shared intimate fellowship from all eternity. God was able
to empathize because this suffering was a shared experience. And
if God empathized with Christ, if he made a way for Christ, won't
he make a way for us too?

Certainty #6—When we suffer, it's okay to ask "Why?"

Earlier I said that "Why?" isn't always the most helpful question. But it is usually the most human. We see the humanity of Jesus on display in the garden as he essentially asks, "If there is another way . . . Why is there not another way?"

It's also okay to not understand why we are having to endure suffering. God's ways are not our ways (see Isaiah 55:8–9). And even if God explained what we were going through and gave us his reasoning, it's likely we wouldn't understand, let alone agree with it.

Asking "Why?" does not show a lack of faith but reveals faith. It's acknowledging that God alone has the answers to questions we desperately desire answers to. There may be more from this mountain garden story, but there are at least six certainties that we can hold to and embrace by faith when we walk through dark and lonely times. Let's never trade what we know for what we don't know.

WWJD

Before there were wristbands with messages like "LIVESTRONG" and "I AM SECOND" or whatever motto or company one wanted to represent on them, there was one in Christian circles with four letters: WWJD. The initialism stands for "What Would Jesus Do?"

The phrase comes from Charles Sheldon's classic book *In His Steps*. The book deals with a group of believers who decided to ask this question before they made any decision, no matter how major or minor: "What would Jesus do?" It's a question that's been trivialized over the years, but I think it's a good question to ask when we suffer. After all, if anyone was certain about the purpose and promise of suffering, it was Jesus. On his mountaintop of suffering, Jesus modeled the truths of suffering, but he also modeled exactly what we should do when trying times come our way.

First, *Jesus prayed.* It was not his suffering that prompted him to pray but his desire to connect with his Father. Prayer was as natural as breathing to Jesus. His entire life was a life of prayer. It was in prayer that he heard his Father's will. It was in prayer that he gained inner strength to follow his Father's direction. Prayer was, and is, the secret to making it through the garden.

It sounds simple, but too often we neglect this important discipline, especially when times get tough. It's easier to talk to friends about what we are going through or to isolate ourselves. I've seen a lot of people try to avoid dealing with their pain. They escape their situation by losing themselves in entertainment, or they try to forget the burden on their shoulders by sleeping it away. Some try to remove reality by turning to harmful substances, all the while creating more pain and suffering for themselves and those they love. But when Jesus faced the darkest moment of his life, he turned to prayer.

In those prayers, Jesus was honest. He asked God the Father whether there was another way to guarantee the salvation of the world. There was no pretense, just honesty and transparency. Suffering has a way of stripping us of the facade we sometimes put on in front of people and leaving us bare before the Lord. This is a good thing. This is the type of prayer God wants to hear from us.

Second, *Jesus yielded.* He was honest in his prayers, but he also meant it when he said, "Nevertheless, not my will, but yours, be done." This was not some type of bargaining chip Jesus was using with his Father, or a spineless resignation. This was the true intent of his heart. As much as he wanted a way out, he was committed to the Father's will. He was submissive. Jesus wanted his Father's plans to be accomplished, and if that meant suffering, then so be it. In fact, he endured it willingly, looking forward to the future "joy that was set before him."

When the valley is low and the night is darkest, let's look to Jesus and model exactly how he responded to suffering rather than trying to get out of it. We pray. We yield. And we endure. In this, we will discover the proximity of God. (See Psalm 34:17–18.)

In the mountain garden, we can gain a new perspective on God's nearness, his ultimate desire for our good. In the mountain garden we will see that he's not abandoned us. There he will prove he is beside us, in the garden, closer to us than we could have ever imagined. After all, he is Immanuel: God with us.

Moving Ahead

Suffering so often brings us closer to Christ. It strips us of nonessentials, causing us to think about what is really important. What is eternal.

If you ask Steve and Lisa Higgs, they would do anything to change the outcome of the events that led to Bo's death all those years ago. I know I would. I miss my friend and think about him all the time. Those of us who loved Bo suffered a great loss, and the sting of that death continues to this day, especially for his family.

They've been in the valley. They know what it's like to go through the dark night of the soul. It's been a tough journey, and it still is. But they would also tell you that Jesus is faithfully near. They would also tell you they met their Savior in the suffering and that they look forward to heaven now more than ever. The thought of sitting with Bo and Jesus makes eternity seem all the sweeter. It wasn't a traditional mountaintop experience—that much is true— but it was a mountain garden experience. And gardens are where things grow, and that includes us.

Mount Calvary

The God Who Is Love

have a recurring meeting with Andrew that happens only when he is ready to meet. I've known Andrew for over ten years. He is gifted in so many ways, good looking and successful. He has great parents and was afforded a great deal of privilege growing up in suburban Dallas. When I first met Andrew, he was eager to jump in and serve our church as an usher and a greeter. Naturally outgoing and gregarious, he fit that role perfectly.

Over time, though, I began to see less and less of Andrew. He wasn't coming to our small groups anymore. I didn't see him at his weekly post, saying hello to people when they came in and helping them find a seat. His parents were still actively involved, and they'd talk about Andrew from time to time, but it was clear he'd dropped off the map.

One day, out of the blue, Andrew reached out and wanted to meet for coffee. It had probably been close to five years since I had seen him, so I was looking forward to reconnecting. We have a nice little coffee shop on our church campus, so I figured this would be a good place for us to meet and catch up. When I walked down to meet Andrew, I was blown away. Had he not stood up and introduced himself, I don't know whether I would have recognized him.

Andrew was clearly not in the best of shape. He had put on some weight. His skin color was pale, and he had dark circles around his eyes. He was not dressed as sharp as I had seen in the past, and while he still had a great smile, it was not nearly as flashy, bright, and quick as before. This was not the Andrew that I remembered.

When we sat down, he began to apologize for not being at church and for getting away from what he knew he should be doing. He told me about his life, how anxiety and an obsessive-compulsive disorder had led him down the road to alcohol. It was his secret sin. And it was pursuing him like a pack of hungry wolves. Over and over again, he would find himself falling to the temptation to drink. It was consuming him. This led, of course, to guilt, which led him to anxiety, which brought on isolation, which led to more drinking. It was a vicious cycle, a confusing loop, and he confessed to feeling as miserable as he looked.

Nothing seemed to help. He had been to professional counselors and psychiatrists. The medicines they prescribed didn't take the edge off his anxiety, plus he didn't like the way they made him feel. My heart broke seeing Andrew like this. He was a mess, a shell of the vibrant man whom I knew years before.

I didn't say much as he talked; I just listened. And then he asked me a question that caught me totally off guard. Andrew wanted to know if he had lost his salvation or if he'd ever had salvation in the first place. He couldn't reconcile how he could struggle in sin and not beat this addiction if God was really living inside him. He went on to tell me that this was the very root of his anxiety. And he drank and drank as a way to avoid the pain of wondering about his eternal destiny.

I hated hearing about the pain Andrew was going through and seeing the agony that was written all over his face. But something told me there might not be a better place for him to be right then. I sensed he had a mountain to climb, specifically, the mountain known as Mount Calvary.

Holy Ground

Millions of believers every year make the pilgrimage to the Garden Tomb, a site outside the Old City of Jerusalem. It offers a very peaceful setting in the middle of the noisy, bustling city. Near that tomb is a place called "Gordon's Calvary."

In 1863, a British general and staunch believer by the name of Charles Gordon was visiting the Holy Land. He was staying very close to this garden site when he noticed that near to it was a rock quarry on a hill. He saw the outline of a skull formed in the stone in that rock, an outline still seen today. It became known as "Skull Hill," and each time I visit the Holy Land with a group, I wait until the last day of our time in Jerusalem to take them to the site. There we sing, share in the Lord's Supper, and pray together. It is no doubt the highlight of the trip.

It's an amazing tourist destination, this site where many believe Jesus gave his life for the sins of the world. Of course, we don't know whether it's the exact location or not, and it really doesn't matter. What matters is that this exchange—his blood for our sin—took place on the mountain of Christ's execution over two thousand years ago.

If ever there was holy ground, the site of the crucifixion of Jesus has to be it. It goes by a number of different names in the

Bible: "Golgotha" in Aramaic; "Calvary" in Latin ; "The Skull" in the gospel of Luke. Mark's account tells it like this:

> They brought him to the place called Golgotha (which means Place of a Skull). And they offered him wine mixed with myrrh, but he did not take it. And they crucified him and divided his garments among them, casting lots for them, to decide what each should take. And it was the third hour when they crucified him. And the inscription of the charge against him read, "The King of the Jews." And with him they crucified two robbers, one on his right and one on his left. (15:22–28)

There is so much in this passage of Scripture and in the Passion narrative. Whenever I talk or write about the Cross, on that mountain where Jesus was put to death, I fear that people may check out and not listen. I fear, especially in Christian circles, that we have become so familiar with the old, old story that our eyes glaze over. Sometimes we don't really pay attention to the depth of the event. But if we hope to ascend this most holy mountain and get a clearer view of God and ourselves, we must stay awake and stay engaged.

The Peak

Jesus climbed the mountain of suffering and sacrifice. He hung on the cross to pave the way to the forgiveness of our sin and to restore us to a right relationship with God. And in his crucifixion, we see that Jesus suffered *physically.*

You may have heard that there was not a more cruel and inhumane way to kill someone than by crucifixion. But did you know it was so bad that the Romans made it against the law to inflict it on their own citizens? It was a torture no Roman wanted to endure, and in Jesus's case, the torture was especially brutal.

What Jesus went through from a physical perspective is astounding. His crucifixion came on the heels of being beaten and flogged by a *lector,* a professional torturer who was skilled at inflicting pain. He knew precisely how to use various whips and instruments meant to fillet the human body. It was not uncommon for a Roman scourging to be fatal in and of itself. But in Jesus's case, the lector stopped just short. They managed to preserve just enough of his life to hang him on a cross as a public spectacle.

After the flogging, Jesus was forced to carry his cross to the place of his execution. There, they laid him out across the timbers, arms outstretched (probably even pulled out of joint), and his wrists were tied to the cross. Nails were then driven between the radius and ulna, the bones in the forearm, to secure the upper body to the wooden beam of the cross. Next, his feet would have been nailed together left over right and placed on a wooden platform that they would have pushed up to allow the knees to be bent. This positioning of his feet would enable the torture to continue even longer, as it would allow the crucified to push himself up to gather oxygen when his sagging body threatened to collapse his lungs.

This pushing up and sagging down process would happen over and over again until eventually the victim was no longer able to continue. Then asphyxiation would occur and ultimately take the life of the one hanging on the cross.

The Bible teaches that Jesus was on the cross for six hours. To put that in some perspective, the median marathon time is four and a half hours. Jesus endured more than a marathon of the worst physical pain one could imagine. That's the average length of watching three movies or attending two baseball games. This is not even counting his arrest and questioning the night before and the ensuing beating and mocking that took place. If the suffering would have been merely physical, it would have been too much. But Jesus did not just suffer physically. He also suffered *emotionally*.

Think about what Jesus went through leading up to the cross. Judas, one of the twelve disciples, betrayed him and turned him over to the officials. Peter, a member of his inner circle and close friend, denied him, claiming on three occasions that he had never even met Jesus. And according to Mark's gospel account, when Jesus was arrested in the Garden of Gethsemane, all the disciples "left him and fled."

Betrayed, denied, and abandoned, Jesus was then brought before a kangaroo court that made up charges against him. The proposed witnesses' accusations didn't line up and even contradicted one another. Mark's gospel recounts it this way:

> Now the chief priests and the whole council were seeking
> testimony against Jesus to put him to death, but they

found none. For many bore false witness against him, but
their testimony did not agree. And some stood up and
bore false witness against him, saying, "We heard him say,
'I will destroy this temple that is made with hands, and in
three days I will build another, not made with hands.'"
Yet even about this their testimony did not agree.
(14:55–59)

On trumped-up testimony and baseless accusations, Jesus
was condemned, then thrown in a dungeon while he waited to be
paraded the next day before Pilate and Herod. This parade,
though, was just for show. The religious leaders wanted blood.
And they were determined to get it. Early Friday morning, Jesus
was sentenced to death.

Consider the emotional impact of having his creation call for
his execution. Consider, too, the emotional pain of being hit by
hands he knit together at creation, of being spit upon and ridi-
culed by mouths he fashioned and formed. Just think for a moment about the shame of having his creation strip him naked and
gamble for his clothes. What must it have been like to hear the
shouts and cries for crucifixion on Friday from the same people
who had shouted "Hosanna" just five days previously? Surely Jesus
was heartbroken.

But there was still another layer of suffering to be endured,
one on a different level entirely. Try to consider what Jesus went
through *spiritually*.

Jesus had known only the love, affirmation, and approval of

his Father. Not one time in his life was there ever a sense of displeasure or disunity. At the baptism of Jesus, a voice came from heaven: "This is my beloved Son, with whom I am well pleased." In the Transfiguration at Mount Hermon, that same voice came from a cloud, once again saying almost the same thing: "This is my beloved Son, with whom I am well pleased; listen to him." Jesus and the Father were connected, unified.

In the prayer life of Jesus, he always directed his prayer to his "Father." But in the final hours of his life, a noticeable shift took place. Mark recorded,

> When the sixth hour had come, there was darkness over the
> whole land until the ninth hour. And at the ninth hour
> Jesus cried with a loud voice, "Eloi, Eloi, lema sabachthani?"
> which means, "My God, my God, why have you forsaken
> me?" (15:33–34)

It was the moment that God laid on Jesus "the iniquity of us all," which led to a spiritual estrangement between God the Father and God the Son. This was something Jesus had never experienced before. In that moment, he cried out to his estranged Father, and a more literal translation of his cry is "My God, my God, why ME have you forsaken?" This has been referred to as the "cry of dereliction" or the "cry of desertion." The God who is "of purer eyes than to see evil and cannot look at wrong" turned his back on his beloved son. In fact, he turned his back on all humanity in that moment, and as a result, the whole land was covered in physical darkness.

Jesus was not just feeling abandoned by God at Calvary; he *was* abandoned by God. This was nearly more pain than the Son of God could bear.

It was physical, emotional, and spiritual agony that Jesus went through on the cross. The question we are compelled to ask is *Why?* We find our answer by looking to the historic symbol of Christianity, the cross.

Signs and Symbols

Everything today seems to be driven by signs, symbols, or icons. From the Nike swoosh to the golden arches of McDonald's, signs and symbols are a part of our daily lives. At the time of this writing *The Emoji Movie* has just been released, and my kids are begging me to take them. Who knew we would be at a place in life where one small image, one digital emoji, could communicate an entire idea? The marketing departments of our favorite brands have trained us well. We know what something is or what company is represented simply by its logo. This is the power of a simple sign.

The cross is the central symbol of Christianity, and we make much of it. We put it on top of our churches as beacons in our communities. Many wear it as jewelry, and crosses have become decorations in homes. In church we sing songs like "The Wonderful

Cross" and "The Old Rugged Cross." But I wonder whether we ever slow down and really think about what the cross represents?

When was the last time you focused your mind and heart on what took place on Mount Calvary and thought about what the cross really means, what it really says? I invite you to do that with me now. Let's think about what the cross really means, by reflecting on what was nailed to it.

What was first nailed to the cross was a *sign*. John recorded for us,

> There they crucified him, and with him two others, one on either side, and Jesus between them. Pilate also wrote an inscription and put it on the cross. It read, "Jesus of Nazareth, the King of the Jews." Many of the Jews read this inscription, for the place where Jesus was crucified was near the city, and it was written in Aramaic, in Latin, and in Greek. So the chief priests of the Jews said to Pilate, "Do not write, 'The King of the Jews,' but rather, 'This man said, I am King of the Jews.'" Pilate answered, "What I have written I have written." (John 19:18–22)

In those days, it was customary that before someone was crucified, a messenger would walk in front of the condemned, holding a sign announcing the crime for which that person was being put to death. As the criminal made his way through the streets, people watching the spectacle would see the sign. They would know the exact reason for the execution. Once they got to the place where the cross would stand, the torturers nailed the placard to the top of the cross over the head of the one being crucified.

This was the Romans' attempt to make very clear what law was broken. They were intent on sending a message to all who watched the crucifixion. Violation of the law would not be tolerated. It was Pax Romana, the peace of Rome, at all costs! Criminals be warned!

The sign that hung above Christ is most interesting because each of the four gospel writers shares the same detail, a rarity in the gospels. In fact, there are only four narratives outside the Passion week that are recorded in all four of the gospels. And even in the Passion week, we find different scenarios, different conversations, and different details. But when it comes to this sign over the head of the cross, each of the gospel writers includes it. But why? Why is the sign so important?

First, consider John's narrative, how he told us it was written in three different languages: Aramaic, the native language of Jesus; Latin, the language of Rome (that is, the world); and Greek, the language of the common people of the day.

The religious leaders wanted Pilate to write "This man said, I am King of the Jews." But the governor was sick of being their puppet. He had already declared on three occasions the innocence of Jesus, saying at one time, "I find no guilt in him." Tired of their games, he said, "What I have written I have written." So, unlike other signs of the day, there was no crime listed above Jesus's head.

It is a testament to his innocence, to the fact that he really was the sinless Son of God. And Pilate knew exactly what he was doing. What he'd written on the sign was meant to be a dig to the Jewish religious leaders of the day and to get under their skin. And sure enough, it did. In a sort of double whammy, it also added to the mockery and shame experienced by Jesus that day.

Pilate didn't know the truth he was declaring: Jesus is a King. Without realizing it, Pilate was the first to declare the kingship of Jesus in a language that all could read and understand. It was the first translation of the gospel message. And one of the first people to read it, a thief who was dying next to Jesus, responded to that message, saying, "Jesus, remember me when you come into your kingdom."

Upon the cross was nailed the first announcement of the kingship of Jesus. Next they nailed Jesus himself to the cross.

The physical, emotional, and spiritual pain and agony Jesus endured were all represented on the cross. And he did all this to save us from sin and reconcile us to God. There was no way around it; Jesus had to shed his blood and die on the cross. It was not only his mission to come and die, but it was also a part of the plan and will of God. Peter preached at Pentecost, "This Jesus, delivered up according to the definite plan and foreknowledge of God, you crucified and killed by the hands of lawless men" (Acts 2:23).

And though the Romans hung him on those beams, Jesus allowed the Crucifixion. In fact, he taught that he willingly laid his life down:

For this reason the Father loves me, because I lay down my
life that I may take it up again. No one takes it from me,
but I lay it down of my own accord. (John 10:17–18)

Jesus went to the cross and became sin for us. He took our sin
and in his substitutionary death absorbed the wrath of a holy God
for us. His blood was poured out as a sacrifice on our behalf because "without the shedding of blood there is no forgiveness of
sins" (Hebrews 9:22).

And this leads to the third observation of what was nailed to
the cross. If you had been on Mount Calvary that day, you would
not have seen this with your physical eyes. It was hidden. But if we
look intently enough at the cross and the One who hangs on it, we
will see something else nailed there. Do you see it? Look harder.
Think deeper. It's our—*sin*.

You, who were dead in your trespasses and the uncircum-
cision of your flesh, God made alive together with him,
having forgiven us all our trespasses, by canceling the
record of debt that stood against us with its legal demands.
This he set aside, nailing it to the cross. He disarmed the
rulers and authorities and put them to open shame, by
triumphing over them in him. (Colossians 2:13–15)

The Bible teaches that on the day when Jesus died, "all" our
sin was nailed to the cross. And don't miss that word *all*. It means

exactly what it says. Regardless of language, *all* means "all." *All* our sin was nailed to the cross.

Our lusts.

Our racism.

Our bitterness and jealousy.

Our anger and rage.

Our immorality.

Our pursuit of idols.

Our impure motives.

Our impure ambitions.

Every evil thought we've ever had.

Every selfish bent we've ever leaned toward.

Sins of omission and sins of commission, sins that we willingly embraced and sins that we don't even know we have committed—these stand against us as a record of debt in God's ledger. And God in his holiness requires sin to be paid for. What is the payment for those sins? According to God's law, sin always demands two things: judgment and death.

The wages of sin is death, but the free gift of God is eternal life in Christ Jesus our Lord. (Romans 6:23)

Death is what our sin deserves. Period. Full stop. End of sentence. We have a record that stands against us, one that must be canceled for us to be in a relationship with God. The record of debt and its demands cannot be overlooked, settled out of court, or simply dismissed. No, it must be canceled and destroyed. Jesus accomplished this when he took *all* our sin and the consequences of judgment and death that came with it.

On the surface, we look at the cross and are tempted to think that it stands only for these things: judgment and death. But when we take a deeper look, we find that the cross is really a symbol of God's love. This was the motive behind Jesus enduring the physical, emotional, and spiritual pain of the cross. Love is what we see when we think long and ponder the cross of Christ. Why the cross? It's clear: the love of God.

The cross is a powerful symbol that communicates to the world an incredible message of hope. It shares the message of a King who loved us so much that he took our place of judgment so that we might enter his kingdom.

Judge Jesus

For as long as I can remember, there have been court-based reality shows on television. When I was growing up, it was *The People's Court*. I never watched that many episodes because, as a child, I would have found it more fun to watch paint dry than watch courtroom drama. For the last twenty-one years, *Judge Judy* has ruled from her throne of justice, making arbitration between parties. And she has made her show a Jerry Springer–type spectacle. From pointed questions and calling out the ignorant to embarrassing verbal lashings, Judge Judy has locked up not only great ratings but also an Emmy.

For the longest time, I thought of Jesus like Judge Judy. He sat on his throne in heaven, and I brought my sin, actions, and motives before him. If I was confessing sin, I would sheepishly creep into his presence, knowing how disappointed he was going to be in me. If it was a certain habitual sin, I would avoid his presence entirely and give it some time. I knew that he wouldn't forget about it completely, but at least after I went through a period of self-loathing, he'd be more apt to extend forgiveness.

On the flip side, when I did what I thought I was supposed to be doing—spending time alone with him, worshipping in community with other believers, serving him by serving others—I was quick to stand before Judge Jesus. He would applaud my efforts and be proud of me.

What I found over time was that my walk with the Lord looked more like an EKG heart-rate chart than it did a steady progression of walking in step with him. If I was doing well spiritually, according to my man-made standards, I felt great. "Hey, look how good I'm doing, how strong in the faith I am!" It led to great pride.

If I was doing poorly, according to my man-made standards, I felt like a failure. This led to a sense of isolation and despair. As I looked at my life, I was vacillating between pride and despair, living off my feelings. It was exhausting, a kind of slow death.

It's true that Jesus is a judge. We can't just strike this attribute from him. It's inherent in his character; it is who he is. However, the other side of that coin is that Jesus is love. And that's what I saw when I began to look deeply into the cross.

Seeing God as he truly is—the loving Father who made a way

for me—resulted in a change in the way I see myself, in the way I live. I haven't completely arrived, but I am trying each day to no longer live to check off a list of moralistic behaviors that I think make me right with God. I have discovered that I do not need to live in fear of losing God's approval. Because of Jesus and what took place at Mount Calvary, I am already approved. Jesus won my approval on the cross. A hard new look into the cross showed me that because of what Jesus did there, I am already right with God.

What clicked for me and finally led to victorious Christian living was when I began to trust the work of Christ on the cross and what God's Word said about my identity through that cross. I began to trust the truth instead of my feelings. I learned that while feelings come and go and are based on circumstances— particularly feelings of approval and disapproval—truth remains constant. It is the truth that I have to base my life on and live by.

This way of thinking changed everything for me. I no longer live in fear. I no longer live in doubt. I no longer waver between pride and despair. In Christ and his accomplished work on the cross, I am forgiven, accepted, loved, and made free by the King. Even when I'm not feeling it. This is why the gospel is called good news.

The Caboose

Andrew recently got out of rehab and is on the up-and-up. He knows that alcohol dependency, anxiety, and cycles of guilt and shame are things he'll battle day by day. The last time we met, he wanted me to assure him once again that God had not given up on him, that he was a Christian in spite of his failures and inadequacies.

I talked with him about his need to base his life on the truth of God's Word and not on how he felt. I have some old discipleship material that I often take people through. I draw an image of a train. I did this for Andrew that day. The first car of the train, the engine, represented truth. Who Andrew is in Christ and what God's Word says about his identity as a child of God is the engine that should drive his life. The last car was the caboose, which represented Andrew's feelings. Feelings are valid and worth our attention. But I told Andrew they couldn't run his life. Every caboose I saw as a child brought up the rear. Truth always precedes feelings and emotions.

I pleaded with Andrew to take the journey to Mount Calvary and to stare into the cross. I wanted him to see Jesus nailed there and to look even deeper to see his sin nailed there too. I told him to gaze at it until he saw the truth and his feelings finally followed. Because until Andrew sees Jesus for who he really is and what he has done on the cross, Andrew will never believe who Jesus has made him to be. He'll never experience the abundant life that Jesus has promised him.

I cannot make the climb to Mount Calvary for Andrew. And I can't make it for you. But I can cheer Andrew on. I can cheer you on. Set your mind on the cross. Take a step toward it each day to see Jesus up close. It's here at Mount Calvary you will discover the God who is love and that this God loves you.

The Mountain with No Name

The God Who Sends

've always enjoyed working and writing away from my office. Set me up in a coffee shop and I'm good to go. I'm not a coffee snob either. I don't have to be in the local hole-in-the-wall or a high-end hipster joint. I'm not looking for any specialty sort of espresso drink. Starbucks is fine with me, and whatever they have on drip will suffice if it's as dark as night and bold as the apostle Paul.

Fortunately, they built a Starbucks right across the street from our church. For years now, I've gone there religiously to read, have meetings, catch up on email, and just hang out. When I first started going, a particular barista was clearly the life of any party. As she was always friendly and in a good mood, we hit it off immediately. It didn't hurt that she knew I was a regular and would give me free coffee every now and again.

We grew to be friends, even though we were complete opposites. I'm a pastor, clean cut and wearing just about the same thing every day: button-down shirt and blue jeans. She hated religion and despised that our church was across the street from her place of employment. She had jet-black hair and wore dark makeup on her pale skin. She had more piercings than I could count and sported some vintage black-rimmed glasses that I couldn't get away with in a million years. I loved theology. She loved art. We couldn't have been more opposite.

I never hid from her that I was a pastor from across the street, and to her credit she didn't write me off or keep me at arm's length because of it. After a few weeks of me consistently coming in the shop, we began talking about books, different cultural issues, and current events of the world. Over a period of time and after developing some trust, Julie began to confide in me about a sour relationship she was in. I also learned she had a baby on the way and was trying to "figure things out." I was always forthright in sharing Jesus with her, and while she never flat-out rejected the claims of Christ, she didn't really want anything to do with him.

I never thought of Julie as a project. She was one of my local friends, and I always enjoyed talking with her. Once, while I was meeting with someone, she came by my table and slipped me a note she had written on a receipt. It was perhaps the greatest compliment I have ever been given. The note read,

> Jared, [totally misspelled my name!] you know what it is
> I like about you? You have always had the decency not to
> preach at me. I appreciate that and I think it's fabulous . . .
> after all, the love of Jesus shouldn't be sold like a salesman,
> and when or if I ever find it, it'll mean that much more.
> Thanks, Julie.

I have kept that note as a reminder to always pray for Julie. I always believed that God could use her in amazing ways if she ever decided to commit her life to him.

Mission Statements

Whether it's a business, a school, a church, or even in personal leadership, we're told that to stay on mission, it's important to have a mission statement. At our church, we print it in the weekly worship guide and always keep it front and center:

> Our mission at Prestonwood Baptist Church is to glorify
> God by introducing Jesus Christ as Lord to as many
> people as possible and to develop them in Christian living
> using the most effective means to impact the world,
> making an eternal difference in this generation.

Mission statements are supposed to keep you aligned. They are meant to inspire. They help maintain focus on the purpose of the organization. It's no real wonder why Jesus gave his disciples a mission statement shortly after his resurrection.

> Now the eleven disciples went to Galilee, to the mountain
> to which Jesus had directed them. And when they saw him
> they worshiped him, but some doubted. And Jesus came
> and said to them, "All authority in heaven and on earth has
> been given to me. Go therefore and make disciples of all
> nations, baptizing them in the name of the Father and of
> the Son and of the Holy Spirit, teaching them to observe all
> that I have commanded you. And behold, I am with you
> always, to the end of the age." (Matthew 28:16–20)

For three years Jesus had invested his life in this small band of believers. He taught them. He lived with them. They shared meals together, experienced the good and the bad together. They had climbed a few mountains together, literally and figuratively. And before returning to his Father, Jesus had one more mountain in mind for them. Scripture doesn't name this mountain in Galilee, so we'll call it "the mountain with no name." Mount No-Name. It really doesn't matter. What mattered more was the name these disciples would carry with them and share with the world when they descended this mountain: the name of Jesus.

Can you imagine the number of emotions and thoughts the disciples had at this time? They'd witnessed Jesus die on the cross but then were suddenly sitting across from him eating a meal. It was beyond their wildest imagination. So what was next? Would he deliver God's people from Roman rule and put Israel back on the map? Would he invoke his full authority and put them in charge? They were ready for action and were committed to do whatever Jesus instructed.

And just look at his instruction. He's not giving them a small task here. His mission statement is bold and audacious. Go into the whole world and make disciples. And though many have taught that the clear command in this passage is to "go," a proper reading in the original text proves that the emphasis and command given in this verse is to "make disciples."

Based on the verb tense and wording of the Greek text, Jesus was saying: "As you go, make disciples. As you baptize, make disciples. As you teach, make disciples." The entire thrust of the mission statement Jesus gave is to make disciples. *Making disciples is what changes the world.*

As You Go

While there is both a necessity and an urgency to go into the world and make disciples, not everyone will have the means, resources, or abilities to go to a foreign country. That's why I love the mission statement Jesus gives. We may not be able to cross the oceans to share the gospel, but we can cross the street. It may not be possible for us to walk across certain borders to share the change Jesus has made in our lives, but we can walk down the hall to share with a coworker.

The Great Commission is for everyone. It's for the schoolteacher and coach as well as the brickmason and nurse. Sharing the good news of Jesus and making disciples is the mission for a server in a restaurant or the CEO of a company. As you go about your day, you pray for ways to intentionally share with and invest in the people around you. This is what changes the world; we are all missionaries in the sense. We go every day. And as we go, we pour what we have learned and know into others: *this* changes the world.

I've got a friend who lives for the mission of making disciples. He is a professor in a university but sees his classroom as his own mission field. He sees his students not as nameless kids taking classes in order to graduate but as people loved by God. He strives to show them the love of Christ in how he engages them inside and outside the classroom. He also enjoys cycling. He sees every group he trains in or race he signs up for not just as accountability to help him get better as a cyclist, but as opportunities to share what God is doing in his own life. He loves to help and encourage others. He is helping our church rethink how we disciple new believers because he knows what it's like to be a baby Christian and how important those first few weeks as a new believer are. Discipleship is not a program to him; it's a way of life. Everywhere he goes is an opportunity to share Jesus and invite others to join him on his journey.

Really only one thing is required of us to participate in the mission Jesus gave us: action. Jesus, sharing a sweet mountaintop moment with his closest friends, made it clear: mountaintop moments don't last forever. Mountaintops are meant to inspire us to action, to go where the people are. And this was the heart of Jesus's message in the Great Commission.

He calls us to the mountains. Here he moves in our hearts, teaches and shows us something of his character and nature. Then we return to where we came from to share with others what he has spoken and shown us on the mountaintop.

In pastoring and meeting with people over the years, I have found one major reason for inaction, for why we are hesitant to share down in the valley what we learned on the mountaintop. It's fear. Fear of what people would think. Fear of being rejected. Fear of not saying the right thing. Fear of not having an answer to a question that may be presented to us.

Jesus knew that in taking his message to the world, fear would be present in our lives. After all, it was Jesus who taught about the cost to follow and obey him. If we take him up on his command to go and make disciples, Jesus warned that we could get into more than our fair share of trouble He made it clear that our decision to obey him has the potential to divide homes, separate close friends, and even in extreme cases cost us our lives.

Making disciples would not be easy. Fear would be inevitably present. But sharing Jesus and making disciples is the only mission the church was given.

Yes, It Takes a Village

Through the years, I have come up with my own definition of discipleship. It is the developmental process of teaching people to be more like Jesus. It takes place when one believer passes on to someone else what he or she knows, has experienced, and has learned. This is what it means to truly make disciples. And it all happens within the context of relationships. Paul put it like this to his disciple Timothy:

> You then, my child, be strengthened by the grace that is in Christ Jesus, and what you have heard from me in the presence of many witnesses entrust to faithful men, who will be able to teach others also. (2 Timothy 2:1–2)

The word *entrust* carries the idea of depositing something of value in a bank for safekeeping. When we come to know Jesus, he deposits within us the good news of his death, burial, and resurrection. He entrusts us with this message, and we are commanded to entrust it to others.

A perfect picture of this is a relay race. One runner runs his part of the race, and the other does not begin his race until the baton has safely passed from one runner to the next. This is essentially the picture that Paul gave Timothy and that Jesus gave his disciples.

Paul wrote to the church in Corinth, "I planted, Apollos watered, but God gave the growth" and that they were all "God's fellow workers." For Paul, making disciples was a team sport. He taught that we all have a part to play in the mission of Christ.

I love thinking about the people who walked off their mountains with Jesus, who came into my life and passed the baton of faith to me. I would not be where I am today if my great-grandparents had not passed their faith on to my grandparents, who passed it on to my parents, who passed it on to me. If it were not for Mrs. Joyce Shoebridge taking over my Sunday school class when I was in the sixth grade and staying with my class through my senior year of high school, there is no way I would be the person I am today. She taught me every Sunday, led me through Bible studies like the Blackaby study *Experiencing God,* and called me out when my priorities were off or out of balance.

I think about people like Mike Fechner. When I graduated college and began ministry, he immediately took me under his wing and discipled me. He had a heart for the inner city and would take me into the hood of South Dallas where he shared his faith and met the needs of a community that needed attention and love. He showed me what it was to give sacrificially and took me in as a part of his family. Mike led by example in breaking down racial barriers and taught me to live by faith.

It's people like my pastor, Dr. Jack Graham, who believed in me and gave me opportunities for leadership. He has modeled for me what biblical preaching looks like and showed me how to lead from a place of integrity.

I could go on and on naming people in my life who have entrusted to me the gospel message. I'm grateful they came off the mountaintop of their experiences with God and came back down into the valley to walk alongside me and invest their lives in me. I've learned through the years that mountaintops are wonderful to visit but nobody lives there. Eventually, we all have to come down. Why not come down and share with others what God taught us there?

Peanut Butter and Jelly

For as long as I can remember, I have loved peanut butter and jelly sandwiches. If I want to frustrate my wife, all I have to do is tell her to cook dinner just for the kids because I am going to eat a PB&J for dinner. To me, there is just nothing better. Add a cold glass of milk to it, and I am one happy man. And whether you mix the peanut butter and jelly before you put it on the sandwich or separate each on its own piece of bread, it makes no difference to me. Just give me the PB&J. Something magical happens when you put these two ingredients together.

When it comes to the Great Commission, the call to "go . . . and make disciples" is sandwiched between two incredible promises. One side is the peanut butter and the other side the jelly. When you put these two promises together, you have something special. The first promise is found when Jesus said, "All authority in heaven and on earth has been given to me."

The word *all* is a key to understanding this passage in its fullness. It's used four times in this passage of Scripture. The idea behind this verse is that Jesus, because of his identity as the resurrected Son of God, has all the right, power, and authority in this world and the world beyond. Everything revolves, is filtered, and takes place according to his divine prerogative. Because he died for the sins of the world and was raised to life, no one else has the position or authority that Jesus holds.

And because he has this authority, he has the right to ask of us whatever he desires. Because of his authority, our only option as his followers is to obey. There is an intimate connection between authority and obedience. This is true in terms of our relationship with Christ, and it is true in terms of our everyday lives.

Football season is just beginning as I write this chapter. A head coach has all the authority over a football team. More often than not, he holds this position because he has the knowledge, skill, and experience to be in his position. As the head coach, he knows what is right and best for the team, and his philosophy on football provides direction for his team. As the head coach, he has the right to call whatever play he wants. His players, because they are under his authority, run the play that the coach calls.

In the same way, Jesus, our head coach, has made the call to "go . . . and make disciples." Our job as his players, under his authority, is to implement and execute what he has called us to do. As players in God's kingdom, we don't have the right to change the play that's been called or cite excuses as to why we can't carry out the game plan.

The other side of the PB&J is another promise. Jesus said, "Behold, I am with you always, to the end of the age."

On one side, we have the promise of Christ's authority. On the other side, we have the promise of his presence. Put these two ingredients together and, like a PB&J, you have something special.

A better translation of this verse is "I am with you all your days." Jesus has promised that as we travel down the mountain, as we go and make, baptize, and teach disciples, he will be right there with us. What an incredible motivation to fulfill the mission statement that Jesus has called us to.

We know that in every situation we find ourselves in, Jesus is with us and has promised to never leave us. In this process of going into the world and making disciples, we may be persecuted, let down, and disappointed. It may cost us some time and some inconvenience. We may not find ourselves in what we would describe as our comfort zone. But we know that Jesus has all authority and is therefore in complete control. We know that he is always with us, always present to guide and help us as we carry out what he has asked of us.

In giving us these two promises, he is taking away every excuse, hesitation, and fear we have about not fulfilling the mission he has given us.

On this unnamed mountain, we find that the Christian life is not meant to be a solo climb in order to meet with God and remain in some kind of holy huddle atop that mountain. Instead, it's on this mountain that our hearts and visions are enlarged to see how great the love of God is, and how much a lost and hurting world needs to experience it. We are forever changed, and as we go back down the mountain, we are compelled to share with others this message of hope that has affected us in such incredible ways. We leave the mountain on mission.

Where the People Are

For months, I pulled Julie's note from my desk and prayed for her. One day, quite unexpectedly, Julie called me and said, "You are never going to believe what happened." She told me that she was up late reading the Bible and something happened on the inside. She immediately called a friend who was also a Christian and told her what was taking place in her heart. Her friend drove over to her house to listen to her and counsel her. After a few hours of discussion and tears, Julie asked Jesus to save her. She wanted me to know. And she was right. I couldn't believe it.

I had the privilege of baptizing Julie into the faith a few weeks later. To see where God has taken her and what he is doing in her life is amazing. God gave her a new vision for her life. She read the Great Commission and knew she had to follow Jesus wherever he called.

Julie not only led her daughter to Christ but has been a faithful witness for Jesus for a number of years now. She loves sharing her faith and making disciples, so much so that now she is preparing to serve Jesus in Italy and live as a full-time missionary there. She experienced Jesus on the mountain. And as beautiful as that was and continues to be, she knows the life she was saved for is best lived down in the valley. Down where there are coffee shops and elementary schools and retirement centers and shopping malls and baseball fields.

Think about your life, the people around you. At work. At the gym. Those in your neighborhood. Have you ever wondered who God is sending you to share his good news with? Start by looking around. Because that is where the people are.

The Last Mountain

The God Who Is Returning

Several years ago, I made a mistake that I vowed I would never make again. I went to Disney World in the summer. To this day I don't know what I was thinking. In some ways, I guess I was trying to outdo my childhood vacations, which consisted of going to Branson, Missouri, every year. There is only so much fun a kid can have attending country western and variety shows with his parents. I would find out in my one trip to Disney World one of the reasons my parents probably never took me there.

The number of people—I could not believe the number of people. India is the only place I've ever seen with more people per square foot than Disney World. Plus, I was not prepared for the heat, the waiting in lines, the crammed buses, or the emotional outbursts and breakdowns of my kids. And while I wanted them to see all the characters and have a good time, to me the best sight was seeing Disney World in the rearview mirror as we left that day.

If my kids are ever going to experience Disney World again, it will be by way of an invitation to go with a friend, or as would happen in my case, the in-laws would take them. Wanting all four of their grandkids to experience the magic of Disney and well aware of my experience years previously, my wife's parents invited us all on a Disney Cruise. I was hesitant. One, because there would be nowhere to go if I was overwhelmed by the crowds. I guess I could jump. Second, I had never been on a cruise before. I was certain I would run out of things to do by the end of day one. While getting ready to board the ship, I was not sure my story was going to end like the Disney stories usually do: *"And they lived happily ever after."*

Get to Work

The physical, literal return of Jesus is an essential tenet of the Christian faith. It is a nonnegotiable to those who believe the words of the Bible. We can certainly debate issues like the timing of his return and what will happen before or after his return, but we can't debate the fact that Jesus is physically returning to the earth.

Consider these biblical statistics:

- One out of every thirty verses in the Bible speaks of the return of Christ or the end of time.
- Twenty-three of the twenty-seven New Testament books speak of Jesus's return.
- There are 109 prophecies in Scripture referring to the first coming of Jesus and 329 prophecies referring to Jesus's second coming.[9]

Like his first coming, his second coming is certain to happen. What's more, Jesus spoke very clearly about his return, including multiple times in the book of Revelation alone. Consider how John captured the words of Christ:

I am the Alpha and the Omega, . . . who is and who was and who is to come, the Almighty. (1:8)

Behold, I am coming soon. Blessed is the one who keeps
the words of the prophecy of this book. (22:7)

Before his ascension from Mount Olivet, Jesus told the disciples to go back to the city of Jerusalem. They were to wait for the
Holy Spirit to come upon them because only then would they be
empowered to fulfill this great mission he had just given them.

After Jesus challenged them to be his witnesses in the whole
earth, the book of Acts tells us,

When he had said these things, as they were looking on,
he was lifted up, and a cloud took him out of their sight.
And while they were gazing into heaven as he went,
behold, two men stood by them in white robes, and said,
"Men of Galilee, why do you stand looking into heaven?
This Jesus, who was taken up from you into heaven, will
come in the same way as you saw him go into heaven."
Then they returned to Jerusalem from the mount
called Olivet, which is near Jerusalem, a Sabbath day's
journey away. (1:9–12)

I love the picture of the disciples gazing into heaven from the
top of a mountain. It's exactly what I would be doing.

Imagine seeing the resurrected Jesus ascending into heaven, as
if pulled up by invisible wires. Wouldn't you stand still staring up
into the sky too? Then imagine two men appearing, apparently

angels, and telling you to stop standing around and staring up into the sky. "It's time to get to work!" they say.

We'll Leave the Light On

On this mountain, the disciples had a perspective shift: God was inviting them, weak as they were, into his work in the world. They were to leave the mountain and start working toward fulfilling the Great Commission as they awaited Jesus's return. But waiting for the Lord is not a passive "staring into the sky" waiting; instead, it's an active waiting. It's what I call a Motel 6 kind of waiting.

Motel 6 had a great commercial campaign a few years ago. The narrator announced at the end of every commercial, "We'll leave the light on for you." The hotel chain was communicating that no matter how late you arrived, they would be up and waiting on you. You wouldn't find them sleeping on the job. Jesus said this is how we should wait for him to return. We should anticipate it and eagerly wait for it. He gave a parable about this in Luke's gospel, concluding it with these words:

> Stay dressed for action and keep your lamps burning, and
> be like men who are waiting for their master to come home
> from the wedding feast, so that they may open the door to
> him at once when he comes and knocks. (12:35–36)

We can't fall into the trap of thinking that just because this promise was made two thousand years ago and hasn't yet been fulfilled, it's not going to happen. Peter, one of those disciples on the mountain, warned against this type of mind-set:

> Do not overlook this one fact, beloved, that with the Lord one day is as a thousand years, and a thousand years as one day. The Lord is not slow to fulfill his promise as some count slowness, but is patient toward you, not wishing that any should perish, but that all should reach repentance. But the day of the Lord will come like a thief, and then the heavens will pass away with a roar, and the heavenly bodies will be burned up and dissolved, and the earth and the works that are done on it will be exposed.
>
> Since all these things are thus to be dissolved, what sort of people ought you to be in lives of holiness and godliness, waiting for and hastening the coming of the day of God. (2 Peter 3:8–12)

And because none of us know the exact time that Jesus is returning, we're motivated to keep carrying out the work. Peter used the return of Christ as an argument for living in holiness and with a sense of urgency. It drove him to live a life separated from the world and to live with the end in mind.

Reward or Regret

When we have been to the mountain and experienced God, we want everyone to come to the mountain with us. To see what we have seen. To encounter what we have encountered. Not only do we want people to be free of sin and earthly pleasures that don't have lasting value, but we also want to stand ready to give a good account of our work to our returning King.

When Jesus returns, he promises to reward some and to rebuke others. It all depends on what we are found doing at his return. The second coming of Jesus forces us to ask this question: Will we be working faithfully to fulfill the mission he has given us? We will stand before God one day and give an account of our lives.

Some will stand before God with great joy because they gave of themselves and worked to build and advance the kingdom of God. They worked to bring others to their own mountaintop experiences of Christ.

But for others, this day will be a day of deep regret and tragic loss. Paul described this day of standing before Jesus, when our words, works, and even our motives will be seen for what they truly are:

> If anyone builds on the foundation [Jesus] with gold, silver, precious stones, wood, hay, straw—each one's work will become manifest, for the Day will disclose it, because it will be revealed by fire, and the fire will test what sort of work each one has done. If the work that anyone has built on the foundation survives, he will receive a reward. If anyone's work is burned up, he will suffer loss, though he himself will be saved, but only as through fire. (1 Corinthians 3:12–15)

The promise of rewards should give us a holy incentive to live for Jesus until he comes. We are to work faithfully toward accomplishing the mission he has given us.

When I read these passages of Scripture, they cause me to pause and ask the question, Am I just standing around waiting for another mountaintop experience with God, or am I rolling up my sleeves and getting to work?

Happily Ever After

On the Disney Cruise, all my girls got their pictures taken with the Disney princesses. As a dad of all girls, I assure you I have seen every Disney princess movie there is. If forced to, I could even sing the songs. I've got the movies down, and really, when you think about it, it's not that hard because most of the plots are the same. Each involves a princess. The princess is guaranteed to fall in love, but typically there is someone standing in the way, attempting to block true love from running its course.

There is always a curse involved that threatens the life of the princess and the potential relationship that is being pursued. However, toward the end of the movie, the conflict is resolved, someone saves the day, and true love ensues. All the Disney princess movies I've watched end in the exact same way: "And they lived happily ever after."

I love how these stories end, but "happily ever after" never happens without a curse being lifted. Whether it's Prince Naveen and Tiana in *The Princess and the Frog* or Princess Anna and Queen Elsa in *Frozen,* no one lives happily ever after until an act of true love takes the curse away.

In the same way, we labor under the curse of sin and death. But Jesus has promised us that one day he will take the curse totally and completely away. It will happen when he returns to the earth to establish his rule and reign forever. And where will he return? To the mountain he ascended from. It's the ultimate mountaintop experience:

> Then the LORD will go out and fight against those nations
> as when he fights on a day of battle. On that day his feet
> shall stand on the Mount of Olives that lies before
> Jerusalem on the east, and the Mount of Olives shall be
> split in two from east to west by a very wide valley, so
> that one half of the Mount shall move northward, and
> the other half southward. . . . Then the LORD my God
> will come, and all the holy ones with him.
> (Zechariah 14:3–5)

Only when Jesus returns to the Mount of Olives and sets up his earthly kingdom will we live happily ever after. Until that time, God will continue to invite us into his presence to experience him. He is waiting for us to ascend the mountains to know him more intimately and to grow stronger in our relationship with him. He will continue to call us upward to his voice. When we answer, when we start the climb, he will change our perspective of who he is and who we are. Are you ready? The mountains are still calling. God is still calling. The question is always "Will I go?" Will you go? There is not a better time to start the climb than right now.

Climbing Exercises

The Mountains Are Calling

ave you ever tried a ropes course or attempted to make a steep climb up a mountain with an exhibition group? If you have, you are well aware that a guide is there to help lead the way. The guide shows you how the equipment works, explains what verbiage to use in order to communicate, and points out obstacles along the path. Guides have made the journey before. They are experienced and know the mountain intimately. They have a responsibility to get people up and down the mountain safely and to help those making the climb enjoy their trek.

Guides didn't become guides overnight, though. It takes training and requires hard work in order to get to a point where they can help others make the climb for themselves. This is why I have included Climbing Exercises as a part of this book. These exercises will help you digest what you read in each chapter, and hopefully you will become a guide to help others up the mountains.

My goal for you is that you would do the exercises yourself, then take a small group from your church or gather some of your friends and make the journey up the mountains together. Climbing is more fun when you go with your friends, and you will find that you will learn from one another along the way.

Each chapter exercise will contain a quote from the chapter, a few facts, and a variety of thoughts, reflections, and questions. Strive for honesty as you move through these exercises. Space is provided for writing down your responses. Why write them down? Those in the know tell us that our short-term memory retains information for only three minutes; unless it is committed to paper, we can lose an idea or thought forever. Let's begin our climb.

Chapter 1

And I Must Go

> *If you have been a follower of Jesus for very long,*
> *you know what I mean by that term*
> *"mountaintop experience." It's a high mark*
> *in your walk with the Lord.*

When did you first become a follower of Jesus? Were you young or not so young? What was the setting: a church service, summer camp, maybe even a friend's kitchen table? Do you remember any specifics that you heard in that experience, possibly a verse or story the speaker emphasized, or a song that was particularly meaningful to you at the time?

_____
_____
_____
_____
_____

Now recall your most recent mountaintop experience. How long ago was it? Where did it take place? Describe the overall experience in two or three sentences.

_____
_____

_____

_____

_____

In those mountaintop experiences, God is constantly trying to change our perspective of (1) who he is and (2) who we are. Think back on that most recent time. How was your perspective of God changed or challenged? How about your perspective of yourself?

_____

_____

_____

_____

_____

What did you take away from that experience as you descended the mountain? Has it stayed fresh in your heart and mind, or has it faded with a little time?

_____

_____

_____

_____

Chapter 2

Mount Moriah:
The God Who Is Provider

Orientation: Mount Moriah
- Hebrew for "ordained by the Lord"
- Latin Vulgate translates as "land of vision"
- Elevation: 2,520 feet
- The Temple Mount sits atop Mount Moriah.
- Thirty-seven-acre tract of land where the Jewish temple once stood
- Profoundly sacred area to Christians, Jews, and Muslims
- Muslims believe that the remains of the sacrifice of Ishmael can be found here.
- Some scholars will make the claim that Mount Moriah is the same location as Mount Calvary/ Golgotha. The thinking here is to connect Father-Son sacrifices of Isaac and Jesus.
- Specific appearances in the Bible: Genesis 22:2 (main text), 2 Chronicles 3:1 (Solomon building the temple)

On the mountain, we find that [God] is not a demanding ruler, a god of requirements with a short fuse. He's not heartlessly putting us through tests, seeing whether he can cause us to stumble.

How much do you agree with that quote? Use a scale of 1 to 5, with 5 being "I wholeheartedly agree" and 1 being "I really struggle to believe that." Bring to mind a recent experience that would illustrate your score.

_____

_____

_____

_____

_____

Ponder that lyric from the song played at Michael Krol's funeral: "Take this world and give me Jesus." Is that line something you could say with a great deal of certainty? Why or why not? Again, remember to strive for honesty.

_____

_____

_____

_____

_____

Knowing God in a greater way often involves sacrifice. Actually, it always does. What is something you feel God has asked you to give up in order to experience greater closeness with him? Was making that sacrifice easy, hard, or something in between? What have you learned or experienced as a result of making that sacrifice?

_____

_____

_____

_____

_____

Chapter 3

Mount Sinai:
The God Who Is Holy

Orientation: Mount Sinai

- Hebrew for "a bush, enmity"
- Elevation: 7,497 feet
- The vast majority of scholars believe that Mount Sinai and Mount Horeb are the same place due to the description of the delivering of the Ten Commandments in Exodus and Deuteronomy.
- Specific appearances in the Bible: Exodus 19; 24:16; 31:18; 34; Leviticus 7:38; 25:1; 26:46; 27:34; Numbers 3:1; 28:6; Judges 5:5; Nehemiah 9:13; Acts 7:30, 38; Galatians 4:24–25

> *The presence of God was coming to Mount Sinai, and the people had to be prepared for his holiness. Nothing unclean could be on or near the mountain of God.*

Silence. Some people gravitate to it, while others can't stand it. Are you comfortable with silence, or does it always feel alien to who you are? What place, if any, does silence have in your life, specifically in relation to your pursuit of God? Describe what that looks like.

Consider your life right now. What is something that could be considered "unclean," something that is possibly hindering you from experiencing the fullness of what God has for your life? Are you willing to get rid of it? A good first step is to ask for God's forgiveness. Write down the name of a trusted friend whom you could confess this to for accountability's sake.

The chapter mentioned three examples of "things we exchange the glory of God for": **the pleasures of the flesh, the pursuit of success,** and **the approval of man.** If you had to pick one of the three that most reflects your struggle, which one would it be? Try to give an example of what that looks like in your life.

Chapter 4

Mount Carmel:
The God Who Is Trustworthy

Orientation: Mount Carmel

- Hebrew for "God's vineyard"
- Elevation: 1,724 feet
- In ancient times, it was considered asylum hideout for fugitives because of its caves and heavily wooded areas.
- Major tourist attraction in Israel with a statue of Elijah erected upon it.
- Specific appearances in the Bible: 1 Kings 18 (main passage, when prophets of Baal are defeated); 2 Kings 2:25 (Elisha's travels); Song of Solomon 7:5 (used as an illustration); Amos 1:2

> *If there's one thing we learn from the life of Elijah, it's that mountaintop experiences are often preceded by days of being cut down or weeks of melting, being in the fire.*

Recall your most recent season of being in the fire. What was going on during that time? Is it over or still ongoing? What, if anything yet, have you learned during this time?

_____

_____

_____

_____

_____

Compare this most recent season with a time before that when you sensed being "cut down" or "melted." What are the similarities? How about the differences? What lessons did you learn or insights did you gain during that time?

_____

_____

_____

_____

Can you point to a time when you spoke or shared out of your refining season and it benefited someone else? How did that someone respond to you? If not, can you point to a time when someone else shared out of his or her brokenness and it encouraged you? And did you tell the person that it did?

_____

_____

_____

_____

Chapter 5

Mount Desolate:
The God Who Is Intimate

> *If Jesus made the choice to be apart from the crowds and disciples to spend time with his Father, shouldn't I do the same?*

Chances are good you probably hear this question in one of two ways, either as slightly shaming ("I really ought to do better") or slightly grieving ("Yes, I want more time with God"). How do you hear it at the present time? Do you possibly hear it differently than you did in the past? What has changed? And if you hear it as shaming, ask God to show you the truth of his desire to spend time with you as well.

_____

_____

_____

_____

_____

The enemies of intimacy listed in this chapter were **busyness, complacency,** and **comfort.** These three can obviously dovetail a little with one another, but give an example from your life of how each competes with your intimacy with God. Then come up with your own "enemy," and give an example of it in your life.

_____

_____

_____

_____

_____

Take some time to think about your routine spiritually. When do you spend time with the Lord? What does this time look like? Write in the space below a few ways you could grow in this area.

_____

_____

_____

_____

Chapter 6

Mount Eremos:
The God Who Is Father

Orientation: Mount Eremos

- Greek for "uninhabited, deserted"
- Also known as the Mount of Beatitudes
- The traditional location is on the northwest shore of the Sea of Galilee.
- The "Jesus Trail" pilgrimage connects this place to other places in Jesus's life.
- Elevation: 190 feet
- Overlooks the four-mile Plain of Gennesaret, considered by Josephus to be "nature's crowning achievement" because of its famed fertility
- Specific appearances in the Bible: Matthew 5–7 (strongly implied); Luke 6

> *Jesus brought a change of perspective on that mountain. He taught the people that they had access to God and could connect to him as an earthly child would connect to its earthly father.*

What kind of relationship did/do you have with your earthly father? Do you believe that that relationship hinders or helps your relationship with God the Father? What is a specific example that shows the hindrance or the help?

_____

_____

_____

_____

_____

The Lord's Prayer has been and continues to be a constant in the lives of countless Christians around the world:

> *Our Father in heaven,*
> *hallowed be your name.*
> *Your kingdom come,*
> *your will be done,*
>   *on earth as it is in heaven.*
> *Give us this day our daily bread,*
> *and forgive us our debts,*
>   *as we also have forgiven our debtors.*
> *And lead us not into temptation,*
>   *but deliver us from evil.* (Matthew 6:9–13)

It is definitely a simple prayer, but that doesn't necessarily mean it's easy. If you had to pick a line or two that are challenging to pray right now, which ones would you choose, and why? For the next five days, pray just those challenging lines. Ask our Father in heaven for the grace and wisdom needed to navigate those lines in your daily work and relationships.

_____

_____

_____

_____

_____

God has not forgotten you. That is the truth. But has it ever *felt* like he has? Recall an instance when you felt abandoned or even simply overlooked. Were you able to pray during that time? If so, what did that prayer sound like?

_____

_____

_____

_____

_____

Chapter 7

Mount Hermon:
The God Who Is Jesus

Orientation: Mount Hermon

- Hebrew for "sacred mountain"
- Elevation: 9,232 feet
- This mountain range straddles the border between Syria and Lebanon.
- It has three peaks. Because of their height, all three are covered with snow almost year round, which is why it is nicknamed "snowy mountain," "gray-haired mountain," and "mountain of snow."
- It's also nicknamed "the eyes of the nation" in Israel because it was often Israel's primary strategic early warning system.
- The mountain range it is part of extends for nearly ninety-three miles.
- Specific appearances in the Bible: Luke 9:28–36 (main text); Deuteronomy 3:8–9; 4:48; Joshua 12:1, 5; 13:5, 11; Judges 3:3 (geographical references); Psalm 29:6 (as "Sirion"); 42:6; 89:12; 133:3; Song of Solomon 4:8 (used as an illustration); Ezekiel 27:5 (as "Senir")

I love that phrase: unchallenged supremacy. . . .
*It is Jesus alone who commands our worship
and devotion.*

Is Jesus's supremacy unchallenged in your life? Or does he have competition? Don't answer too quickly. Take a few breaths, and see if anyone or anything comes to mind that competes with Jesus. List them all.

_____

_____

_____

_____

_____

Consider your life for a moment. Do you rely heavily on the thoughts and opinions of favorite or popular Bible teachers or preachers? Possibly to the point of not being able to articulate your own thoughts? Remember, the question is not "Who do others say that Jesus is?" but "Who do *you* say that Jesus is?" Right now, in this moment, how would you answer that question?

_____

_____

_____

_____

_____

Chapter 8

Mount Olivet:
The God Who Is Near

Orientation: Mount Olivet

- It is best known for the olive trees that were found there and is located across the Kidron Valley from Jerusalem.
- Elevation: 2,710 feet
- Specific appearances in the Bible: 2 Samuel 15:30; Zechariah 14:4; Matthew 24; Luke 19:29; 21:37; Acts 1:12

> *I share with them a statement of truth that I heard from my pastor years ago: Don't trade what you know for what you don't know.*

Think about a mountain garden experience you've had, something similar to "the dark night of the soul." If you've lived very long, you've had one. Describe it as best you can. Try not to self-edit. If it was dark, witness about the darkness.

_____

_____

_____

_____

_____

Six God-certainties are listed in the chapter. There are no doubt many more, but these are a good start. Out of the six, which one would you point to right now as the most uncertain in your mind? Share the reason for your choice.

1. Suffering is universal and unavoidable.
2. Suffering is not a result of judgment for sin.
3. Suffering is temporary.
4. God loves me and has not forgotten me.
5. God empathizes with me in my suffering.
6. When we suffer, it's okay to ask "Why?"

_____

_____

_____

_____

WWJD: What would Jesus do? How might you begin to incorporate that question into your daily life as it relates to suffering?

_____

_____

_____

_____

Chapter 9

Mount Calvary:
The God Who Is Love

Orientation: Mount Calvary

- Latin *calvarium* means "skull" and Aramaic *Golgotha* means "Place of the Skull."
- Elevation: no universal agreement on location
- Specific appearances in the Bible: Matthew 27:33; Mark 15:22; Luke 23:33 (as "The Skull"); John 19:17

> *I have discovered that I do not need to live in fear of losing God's approval. Because of Jesus and what took place at Mount Calvary, I am already approved. Jesus won my approval on the cross.*

Copy these three sentences down on a notecard, and place them somewhere you'll see them every day for a week. When you see them, read them out loud. And thank God for his indescribable gift.

Read back over the section in this chapter that focuses on the physical, emotional, and spiritual suffering that Jesus endured.

Even though some of the content may be familiar, what stands out to you about those three facets of the Crucifixion?

Physical

_____

_____

_____

_____

Emotional

_____

_____

_____

_____

Spiritual

_____

_____

_____

_____

Take a few moments to reflect on the Cross. Be still and consider God's love for you. Pray and ask God for courage to not live by your feelings, but to help you live out your identity as a child of God.

Chapter 10

The Mountain with No Name:
The God Who Sends

> *I love thinking about the people who walked off their mountains with Jesus, who came into my life and passed the baton of faith to me.*

Start a list of your "village," those people who have invested in you and your walk of faith. If you need more space than is provided here, that's great!

_____

_____

_____

_____

_____

Now you choose the delivery system—a handwritten note, an email, a phone call, whatever—but reach out to one or two who passed the baton of faith to you. Find the words to express your gratitude, even if it is nothing more than these two little words: "Thank you."

Take some time to consider the people in your life, those you know who are younger in their faith journey than you. Ask God to impress on your mind one or two who might need your support, encouragement, or discipleship. Again, you choose the delivery system, but reach out to that one or those two, and connect with them. Commit to pray for them this week.

The Last Mountain: The God Who Is Returning

The imminent return of Jesus helps us live with a sense of urgency because we will live with the end in mind. That sense of urgency is not frantic, fearful living but rather hope-filled, intentional awareness. Is this sense of urgency a familiar feeling for you? How so? In other words, what does it look like in your life? If it's not a familiar feeling, then it is probably uncommon at best or absent at worst. What are two things, just two, that you can do over the next month to foster that sense of urgency in your life? If you're having difficulty coming up with an answer, approach a trusted friend or group of friends, and ask for help in thinking it through.

_____

_____

_____

_____

_____

_____

> *Only when Jesus returns and sets up his earthly kingdom will we live happily ever after.*

Until then, God invites us into a rhythm of ascending alone into the mountains with him and then descending back among our families and friends and colleagues and strangers to live out the truths about God and ourselves that are now clearer to us. But as always, the question is "Will I go?"

Write a prayer of commitment in your own words, asking God for strength to make the climb to meet with him until he comes.

_____

_____

_____

_____

_____

Acknowledgments

There are many people to thank for this project becoming a reality. I'm so grateful to God for calling me to himself while I attended a preteen camp in northwest Louisiana. This was the first of many mountaintop experiences and the one that I treasure the most. There is nothing better than being a follower of Jesus.

To my parents, who have always believed in and supported me in whatever I have been passionate about, thank you. Your examples of hard work, sacrifice, faithfulness, and integrity have been foundational in my life. I am eternally grateful for you and love you deeply.

One of the greatest privileges of my life is serving on the staff of Prestonwood Baptist Church. I am indebted to the people called Prestonwood, and it's a joy to be a part of this faith family. God is allowing me to live a dream in helping pastor this great congregation. Thank you to Dr. Jack Graham for believing in me and giving me a chance. What an honor to serve by your side. To Mike Buster, Jeff Young, Michael Neale, Chris Kouba, and the rest of the staff of Prestonwood, your friendship, encouragement, and support mean more than you will ever know. Also, thank you to Joe Perry for making the call all those years ago inviting me to come be an intern. Shannon Dick, Janis Knight, and Jack Raymond, your assistance in research and offering important feedback throughout the writing process has been incredibly helpful.

Don Gates, you believed in this book from the first time I pitched it to you as an idea. Thanks for running with it and making it happen. Your wisdom, counsel, and advice throughout this journey have been invaluable. Thank you for the opportunity to be a part of the Gates Group. Caleb Kaltenbach, thanks for making the introduction and encouraging me to write what God had put in my heart.

To the great team at WaterBrook Multnomah, thanks for taking a chance on me. John Blase, I am especially grateful to you and Seth Haines for making this book much better than it was when I first turned it in. You have been professional and patient. Thank you for your coaching and expertise. Douglas, Beverly, Kristopher, Pamela, and Lori, thank you for your strategic insights and focused endeavors.

Finally, to Debbie and my girls, Riley, Kelsey, Landry, and Cameron. This book is dedicated to you. Debbie, there is no greater honor than being your husband and the daddy of our girls. I'll go to any mountaintop and walk through any valley as long as you are by my side.

Notes

1. Jason Ingram and Jason Roy, "Where I Belong," *Listen to the Sound,* Provident Label Group, 2011.

2. Harriet Rubin, "Success and Excess," *Fast Company,* September 30, 1998, www.fastcompany.com/35583/success-and-excess.

3. C. S. Lewis, *The Weight of Glory and Other Addresses* (New York: Macmillan, 1949), 2.

4. A. W. Tozer, *The Pursuit of God* (Fairhope, AL: Mockingbird Classics, 2015), vi.

5. Tozer, *Pursuit of God,* 4–5.

6. *NIV Study Bible,* 10th anniversary ed. (Grand Rapids, MI: Zondervan, 1995), s.v. Philippians 2:7.

7. R. V. G. Tasker, *Tyndale New Testament Commentaries: Matthew* (Grand Rapids, MI: Eerdmans, 1961), 164–65.

8. "Christian Persecution," Open Doors, www.opendoorsusa.org/christian-persecution.

9. John Walvoord, "The Second Coming of Christ," Precept Austin, www.preceptaustin.org/the_second_coming_of_christ.

Martyn Whitt[...]er's side) and he was raised o[...]d in Politics from Bristol University, has taught history for over thirty years and is currently the curriculum leader for Spiritual, Moral, Social and Cultural Development at a Wiltshire secondary school. He is the author of thirty-nine books, his most recent being *A Brief History of Life in the Middle Ages* (2009), *A Brief History of the Third Reich* (2011) and *The Viking Blitzkrieg* (2013), the last co-written with his eldest daughter. His specialist area of interest is early medieval British history, the period in which most of the early Celtic myths were first recorded in written form. As well as being a teacher, he is also a Lay Minister in the Church of England. He lives in Wiltshire, in a family where things Celtic and spiritual are high profile, with his eldest daughter working for the devolved Welsh government, his youngest daughter reading Theology at Cambridge and his wife being the daughter of the one-time Methodist minister of Tonypandy, south Wales.